The Constitutional Rights of Children

LANDMARK LAW CASES

&

AMERICAN SOCIETY

Peter Charles Hoffer

N. E. H. Hull

Series Editors

For a complete list of titles in the series go to www.kansaspress.ku.edu

DAVID S. TANENHAUS

The Constitutional Rights of Children

In re Gault and Juvenile Justice

UNIVERSITY PRESS OF KANSAS

Published by the University Press of Kansas (Lawrence, Kansas 66045), which was
organized by the Kansas Board of Regents and is operated and funded by Emporia State
University, Fort Hays State University, Kansas State University, Pittsburg State University,
the University of Kansas, and Wichita State University

Library of Congress Cataloging-in-Publication Data

Tanenhaus, David Spinoza.

The constitutional rights of children : in re Gault and juvenile justice /
David S. Tanenhaus.

p.   cm.

Includes bibliographical references and index.

ISBN 978-0-7006-1813-2 (cloth : alk. paper) — ISBN 978-0-7006-1814-9 (pbk. : alk. paper)

1. Gault, Gerald Francis, 1949 or 50- Trials, litigation, etc. 2. Juvenile justice, Administration
of—United States—Cases. 3. Due process of law—United States—Cases. 4. Children
Cases.—Legal status, laws, etc.—United States I. Title.

KF228.G377T36 2011

342.7308'772—dc22

2011010716

British Library Cataloguing-in-Publication Data is available.

Printed in the United States of America

10 9 8 7 6 5 4 3 2 1

The paper used in this publication is recycled and contains 30 percent postconsumer waste.
It is acid free and meets the minimum requirements of the American National Standard for
Permanence of Paper for Printed Library Materials z39.48-1992.

For Margaret Keeney Rosenheim (1926–2009),

whom Mr. Justice Fortas cited in Gault,

and for Virginia L. Tanenhaus,

who teaches justice to our child,

Isaac Joseph

CONTENTS

There are some law cases where the injustice is so notorious and the indifference of the authorities so casual, that the reader can only scratch his head and ask what was going on. *In re Gault* (1967) seems to be such a case. That an alleged obscene telephone call, unproven (no evidence existed on precisely who made the call or if it was made at all), unsubstantiated (the alleged victim never gave testimony in court and obviously was not cross-examined by counsel), and unrefuted (the suspect did not have the right to confront the accuser, nor were his parents notified in timely fashion), could lead to a young man's incarceration for six years in a house of correction seems a scandalous miscarriage of justice. But the juvenile court judge who handled the case and the Arizona Supreme Court that heard an appeal from his handling of the case agreed that under Arizona law, the discretion of the juvenile court system was unimpeachable. Fifteen-year-old Gerald Gault could be punished far more severely than an adult for an alleged offense with none of the procedural rights the U.S. Constitution guarantees adult defendants.

As in Globe, Arizona, where a neighbor complained that she thought Gault had used obscene language in a telephone call, all over the country juvenile courts exercised similarly untrammeled discretion in a wide variety of juvenile cases. The judges in these courts might or might not be lawyers themselves and might or might not be learned in the law. Designed as a Progressive Era reform to remove juveniles from the adult system's harsh penalties and allow for flexible, child-friendly discretion, by the 1960s the system was a creaking antiquity.

The case arose at a critical moment in the history of juvenile justice. In the 1950s, the problem of juvenile delinquency became the subject of a national debate. Progressive psychological, criminological, and social work authorities were pressing for a more sophisticated and socially aware definition of the problem that would replace older, spare-the-rod-spoil-the-child customs, but local authorities often resisted. Some of the states had introduced modifications in juvenile justice, a standard of "essential fairness" replacing the no-rules of earlier days. But in Arizona, harsh correction, a kind of boot camp for bad boys and girls, was the preferred solution of many juvenile court judges. At these correctional institutions, corporal punishment was common—again subjecting youthful, often first-time offenders to physical harm that adult, more serious offenders did not face in state and federal penitentiaries. Corrupted by the same system, in particular the absence of due process controls on the hearings, some judges in juvenile courts became more arbitrary and tyrannical.

For the Supreme Court, the case came at the end of what constitutional scholars call the "due process revolution," a series of landmark cases in which the Court extended the procedural protections of the Bill of Rights to the states through the "incorporation" of the Fourteenth Amendment's due process and equal protection clauses. These cases included the imposition of a right to counsel (provided by the state if the defendant could not afford to pay), the right to confront accusers, protection against coercion and self-incrimination, and the right to have access to evidence that the prosecution would use in its case. In 1964, U.S. Supreme Court Chief Justice Earl Warren had weighed in on the subject with a plea for reform of juvenile justice. In the same year, Arizona senator Barry Goldwater called for more law and order and less leniency in criminal courts. In a sense, *In re Gault* was an appropriate test and coda to that sweeping reformation of criminal justice practices.

Hidden not very far beneath the surface of the case were vexing questions about the status of children as citizens. Were they, until their majority, actually in the custody of their parents? Did not juvenile courts merely duplicate (or assume) parents' relatively untrammeled discretion in punishing their children? What rights under the Constitution did children have as persons apart from their families? These were questions that went far beyond the possibility of a miscarriage of essential fairness in one juvenile court.

Author David Tanenhaus's informed, elegant, and fully persuasive indictment of "the desert vision of punitive juvenile justice" takes the case from a corner of Arizona all the way to the Supreme Court, and from the frontier-like days after World War II up to the present controversies over strip searches in our schools. He lets the evidence tell its own story, following the words of participants such as the Gault family, Pennsylvania migrants to the copper mining country east of Phoenix. Arizona reformers like Jesse Udall and hardliners like Robert McGhee speak their lines, and we listen in. Lest anyone forget how important it is to have able counsel, Tanenhaus introduces us to Amelia Lewis, the Gaults' attorney, who took on the state of Arizona and its legal officers. Her appeal to the Arizona Supreme Court failed. In the words of Chief Justice Charles Bernstein, himself an early critic of the worst aspects of juvenile justice, the state court agreed that "good intentions do not justify depriving a child of due process of law," but in Gault's case the minimum requirements under the state and federal constitutions had been met.

Lewis then turned to the Northern Arizona branch of the American Civil Liberties Union, and they to the national office in New York. Director Melvin Wulf would take the case to the Supreme Court, and Norman Dorsen would spearhead the litigation. On the Court, newly appointed Justice Abe Fortas was watching closely. As a lawyer, he had developed an interest in juvenile justice reform. But opposition was brewing—federalism, the cost of extending full procedural rights, and the brooding omnipresence of the law-enforcement community raised questions in some jurists' minds about interfering with the juvenile court judges' discretion.

Tanenhaus cracks open the door to the Supreme Court conference room and the chambers of the justices as Justice Fortas labors on his opinion and other justices suggest changes. Is *In re Gault* about a child's rights or his parents' rights? Is it about federal-state relations? We will not reveal how the Court decided the case or local courts' compliance with the decision in later years, but from its first pages to its last, Tanenhaus's retelling is compelling reading and a cautionary tale.

ACKNOWLEDGMENTS

Doing justice to all those who helped me to write this book is a tall order. At the outset, I must thank Peter Hoffer and Michael Briggs for encouraging me to propose the project and for recruiting Barry Feld and Christopher Manfredi to evaluate my proposal. Barry also provided an exceptionally helpful reading of the penultimate draft. I could not have asked for more conscientious editors and readers.

Matthew Wright, the Head of Collections and Instructional Services at the William S. Boyd School of Law, University of Nevada, Las Vegas, and Marianne Alcorn, Head of Reference and Faculty Services, Ross-Blakley Law Library, Arizona State University College of Law, provided indispensable research assistance. I will forever be in their debt. I will also never be able to repay the kindness and support of Dick Morgan, the former dean of Arizona State University College of Law and the founding dean of the William S. Boyd School of Law. Dick not only found space for a historian at a new law school but also provided me with a primer on Arizona legal history and introduced me to former chief justice of the Arizona Supreme Court, Frank X. Gordon, Jr. Dean John Valery White, who succeeded Dick Morgan, and Associate Dean Kay Kindred have continued the law school's tradition of supporting legal history. They approved the summer research grants that made it possible for me to complete this project. Michael W. Bowers, interim executive vice president and provost of the University of Nevada, Las Vegas (UNLV), also took time away from his busy schedule to discuss Arizona law and politics with me. Dean Christopher Hudgins of the College of Liberal Arts has worked tirelessly to ensure that the UNLV History Department remains a green spot in the desert.

My fellow historians Michael S. Green and Mary D. Wammack graciously volunteered to be an audience-in-waiting for even the roughest drafts. Both provided invaluable editorial suggestions on the entire manuscript. Mike also invited me to discuss *Gault* with the students in his UNLV honors seminar on the Supreme Court in American history. Their feedback was encouraging and helpful. I especially appreciated Robyn Raymondo's reflections on growing up near Globe, Arizona. The graduate and law students in my 2009 Children and Society seminar also helped me to develop the concept of desert justice.

Other friends and family members also provided timely and instructive feedback on parts of the manuscript. These attentive readers included Winston Bowman, Al Brophy, Bill Bush, Kathleen Frydl, Joseph "Andy" Fry, Mike Grossberg, Sam Tanenhaus, Virginia Tanenhaus, Beth Tanenhaus Winsten, David Wrobel, and Frank Zimring. My mother, Gussie Tanenhaus, followed the book's progress over the course of our weekly phone calls. I had also a helpful conversation about the book's structure with Don Smith at Grinnell College.

I am thankful to Dan Hulsebosch and Bill Nelson for inviting me to present a draft of chapter 2 at the New York University Legal History Colloquium. The participants helped me to discover the slim book that was struggling to escape from a sprawling mess. I must also thank the late Philip Kurland, a leading critic of the Warren Court. He tutored me in constitutional law during the spring of 1991, teaching me that once you cannot stop thinking about a case, it is time to start writing about it.

My wife, Virginia Tanenhaus, and our son, Isaac Tanenhaus, provided the love and support necessary to write this book with passion. Now that it's complete, I can spend more precious time with them. When I told Isaac that I was nearly done, he asked, "Does that mean that I don't have to go to playschool anymore?" His question reminded me how difficult it is to provide justice to a child. We did, however, reenact *Percy Jackson & the Olympians: The Lightning Thief.* Isaac likes to be Medusa.

{ *Acknowledgments* }

PROLOGUE

The titling of court cases is hardly inspirational. *In re Gault,* 387 U.S. 1 (1967), the official citation for the first U.S. Supreme Court decision to address what elements of due process the Constitution requires in a juvenile court proceeding, is a perfect example. Its title combines a Latin phrase (*in re* = "in the matter of"), a surname (Gault = Gerald Francis Gault, born January 23, 1949), and reference information (i.e., volume 387 of *United States Reports,* beginning on page 1, and published in 1967). This dry title, however, is only the beginning of a remarkable story about how one teenager's legal experiences during the early 1960s in Globe, Arizona, an isolated mining town, ultimately transformed American constitutional law. At that time, fifteen-year-old Gerald Gault, like every other American girl and boy, had no constitutional rights to due process in a juvenile court proceeding, even though a judge could declare him "delinquent" and sentence him to be incarcerated in an "industrial school" until he celebrated his twenty-first birthday. In 1964, the year that the nation's post–World War II baby boom ended, seventy-one million Americans (more than 36 percent of the population) were subject to the jurisdiction of a juvenile court. As FBI Director J. Edgar Hoover testified to Congress, about 4 percent of American youth could expect to find themselves in juvenile court.

The U.S. Supreme Court heard *Gault* near the end of its due process revolution (1961–1968), which nationalized criminal procedure. Beginning in 1961, the Warren Court extended protections in the Bill of Rights, which had previously applied only in federal courts, to the accused and defendants in state criminal courts. In *Gault,* the issue was whether juvenile courts, like adult criminal courts, must protect these constitutional rights, such as the Fifth Amendment's privilege against self-incrimination and the Sixth Amendment's guarantee of assistance of counsel. At the same time that the Supreme Court decided to answer this question, the nation was experiencing an ostensibly terrifying crime wave and persons under eighteen years of age were responsible for more than 20 percent of all police arrests and nearly 50 percent of all arrests for serious offenses. In 1964, juvenile courts committed 39,511 minors, including Gerald Gault, to juvenile prisons. Others were prosecuted as adults in the criminal justice system and sentenced to federal and state penitentiaries. In 1963 alone, for example, criminal courts sent 88,824 persons younger than eighteen years of age to adult prison.

Gault is thus much more than a selection from the canon of American constitutional law. It also invites serious analysis of tough questions about the appropriate legal response to youth crime. How should juveniles who break the law be treated? Should they be tried in the same criminal justice system that prosecutes and incarcerates adults? Or should their cases instead be handled in a separate justice system designed specifically for them? Should adolescents be treated more like young children or more like adults? Should a fifteen-year-old, for example, be punished the same way as either a ten-year-old or a thirty-year-old? Should chronological age, mental capacity, prior record, alleged offense, or life history be factored into making these decisions?

As a historical study of a landmark Supreme Court decision, this book cannot provide definitive answers to such normative questions. Yet the past is a valuable place to begin this conversation. Studying the history of the "juvenile court," which admittedly sounds like a dusty set piece from a Victorian drama, reminds us that crime and the state's response to it are legally defined categories of conduct that have changed dramatically over time. In the American experience, legislatures have primarily defined what is illegal, and appellate courts have used specific cases like *Gault* to define how the state can respond legally to illegality. Thus, this book examines why states initially created juvenile courts at the turn of the twentieth century, and how they operated before and after the U.S. Supreme Court's landmark decision in *Gault*.

On one level, *Gault* is a story of revolutionary constitutionalism. But it is also evidence of the tenacity of localism, often motivated by conservative impulses, in American legal history. In significant ways, the U.S. Supreme Court could not alter the everyday administration of juvenile justice in places like Globe, Arizona. Explaining such persistent continuity is as important as chronicling the radical changes that did occur during the 1960s. This book attempts to do both.

To contextualize *Gault*, from its Progressive Era roots to its recent fortieth anniversary, the book proceeds in three parts. Part I, Desert Justice, examines the pre-history of the case. Chapter 1 begins with a 1952 scandal at the Arizona Industrial School for Boys, popularly known as Fort Grant. By examining the state response to the allegations that the superintendent and his staff had inflicted cruel and unusual punishments on the school's inmates, the chapter describes and analyzes the two competing visions of juvenile justice in post–World War II Arizona. The first vision—progressive juvenile justice—saw juvenile delinquency as primarily a psychological condition that mental-health experts could treat and cure. The second vision—desert juvenile justice—focused on a boy's body, not his mind. Its proponents believed in the efficacy of corporal punishment and imprisonment. Even judges who abhorred the desert vision of punitive juvenile justice had to commit minors to Fort Grant because it was the only secure facility for male juvenile delinquents in Arizona. Gerald Gault spent nearly six months at Fort Grant. Chapter 2 recounts how he ended up in Fort Grant, his parents' legal efforts to free him, and the Arizona Supreme Court's final ruling.

Part II, Legal Liberalism, places the subsequent litigation of *Gault* in its ideological and constitutional contexts. Proponents of legal liberalism believed in using federal courts as agents of change to help historically disadvantaged groups in American society, such as African Americans, women, children, and prisoners. Chapter 3 takes the reader from Arizona to New York City to examine how the American Civil Liberties Union (ACLU), the nation's largest civil rights organization, litigated *Gault* during the heyday of legal liberalism. It examines how ACLU lawyers constructed a legal argument that questioned the Progressive Era assumption that juvenile courts fundamentally differed from criminal courts and should not follow criminal procedure. These lawyers, led by New York University law professor Norman Dorsen, argued that the Fourteenth Amendment required juvenile courts to provide fundamental due process rights during the adjudicatory stage of the process, when a judge determined whether a child was delinquent. The chapter also discusses Arizona's rejoinder to the ACLU's legal theory.

Chapter 4 takes the story from New York City to Washington, D.C., to analyze the oral argument before the justices of the Warren Court on December 6, 1966. It then examines how the Supreme Court decided *Gault*, focusing primarily on Justice Abe Fortas's majority opinion. On May 15, 1967, Fortas famously proclaimed, "Under our Constitution, the condition of being a boy does not justify a kangaroo court." The chapter also analyzes the concurring opinions, Justice Potter Stewart's lone dissent, and initial responses to the decision.

Part III, Just Deserts, explores the contested legacy of *Gault*. Chapter 5 charts changes and continuity in juvenile justice from the aftermath of the decision until the present. In the process, it examines the Supreme Court's subsequent juvenile justice decisions. The chapter concludes that two contexts help to explain the path of the law after *Gault*. First, the ascendancy of conservative constitutionalism, beginning with the Burger Court (1969–1986), ensured that the constitutional domestication of the juvenile court remained incomplete. Thus, the juvenile court ended up as a Progressive Era institution retrofitted with only some basic due process safeguards. Second, although nobody involved in the *Gault* litigation on either side could have predicted it, Americans in the 1970s embraced mass incarceration as a penal strategy. Even though the juvenile court remained a flawed institution, it still spared hundreds of thousands of children and adolescents from this brave new world.

The book concludes with an epilogue about *Redding v. Safford*, a 2009 U.S. Supreme Court decision. The case, originating in 2003 in Safford, Arizona, involved then-thirteen-year-old Savana Redding, who was taken from her middle school classroom and forced to undress before the school nurse and an administrative assistant. The assistant principal believed that she had prescription painkillers in her underwear. This case, especially Justice Clarence Thomas's forceful dissent, reminds us why we should forget neither the Fort Grant scandal nor *Gault*.

The Constitutional Rights of Children

PART I

Desert Justice

CHAPTER I

"A Disgrace for the State of Arizona"

On March 10, 1952, *Time* magazine ran a brief article, "Reasonable Punishment?" that reported this:

> In a state of high excitement, two 17-year-old boys walked into the courthouse of Maricopa County, Arizona. Having served time at the state's "rehabilitation" school at Fort Grant, both had some hair-raising tales to tell. The man they asked to see was Charles C. Bernstein, who presided in the juvenile division of the superior court. If anyone would listen to them, the "kids" judge would. That morning, two months ago, Judge Bernstein did listen—to stories of whippings, blackjackings and assorted cruelties that were hard to believe. But he decided to do some investigating. By last week, he had learned enough to haul Superintendent George R. Ridgway and five of his employees into court in one of the most sordid scandals Arizona has known in years.

Judge Bernstein had filed contempt of court charges against the superintendent and his staff for administering cruel and unusual punishments to wards of the juvenile court.

The Fort Grant scandal was part of the evolving national conversation in the 1950s and 1960s about the causes and extent of juvenile delinquency and what should be done to stop it. Much of the contemporary analysis and angst focused on explaining the dizzying changes in post–World War II youth culture. Teenagers spoke differently than their parents, followed fads in fashion, listened to rock and roll, and appeared to be dancing toward the precipice. The televised hearings of the Senate Subcommittee to Investigate Juvenile Delinquency during the mid-1950s convinced many Americans that a tidal wave of delinquency had washed over the nation and that the purveyors of mass culture—comic books, television, film, and radio—were primarily to blame. The Fort Grant scandal, however, provides a different perspective on the response to juvenile delinquency in the postwar period. Instead of highlighting the concerns over mass culture and the accompanying calls for censorship, it reveals an ongoing struggle among judges, administrators, and legislators for authority and jurisdiction over juvenile justice.

Juvenile justice was a comparatively new area of socialized law that Progressive Era reformers carved out of criminal law at the turn of the twentieth century. Building on the paternalistic idea of the state as a father, embodied in the legal concept of *parens patriae,* the progressive architects of the juvenile court had created a separate court system for juvenile delinquents to treat them as children, not as criminals. As Jane Addams, a leader in the social settlement-house movement who also helped to establish the world's first juvenile court in Chicago in 1899, declared in her book *My Friend, Julia Lathrop:*

> There was almost a change in *mores* when the Juvenile Court was established. The child was brought before the judge with no one to prosecute him and with no one to defend him—the judge and all concerned were merely trying to find out what could be done on his behalf. The element of conflict was absolutely eliminated and with it, all notion of punishment as such with its curiously belated connotation.

By the 1920s, the American juvenile court ideal—that children's cases should be diverted from the criminal justice system and handled in a separate system that emphasized rehabilitation over punishment—had quickly spread across the nation as well as much of the globe. Herbert Lou's *Juvenile Courts in the United States,* which was published in 1927 and remained the standard text in the field through the 1950s, emphasized the benevolence of this approach. Until a "better and finer agency may be evolved," he concluded, "the juvenile court will remain to serve as a fountain of mercy, truth, and justice to our handicapped children."

Progressive Era child welfare experts argued that juvenile court judges required discretion in handling children's cases and should not follow strict criminal procedure such as evidentiary rules. They also insisted that juvenile court judges must be trained lawyers who understood, in the words of Julian Mack, a respected jurist and prominent leader in the movement, that "ours is a government of laws, not of men." In an influential article published in the *Harvard Law Review* in 1909, Mack argued that a juvenile court judge should also "be a student of and deeply interested in the problems of philanthropy and child life, as well as a lover of children." Mack added, "He must be able to understand the boys' points of view and ideas of justice; he must be willing and patient enough to search out the underlying causes of the trouble and to formulate the plan by which, through the cooperation, ofttimes, of many agencies, the cure may be effected." Mack emphasized that it required more than a year of continuous service on the juvenile court bench to acquire the necessary experience to do this vital work effectively.

Yet, as Mack had learned firsthand during his tenure as a juvenile court judge in Chicago, judges could not help the children that they committed to public or private institutions. A judge had autocratic control over his or her courtroom, but that jurisdiction did not extend over juvenile corrections—what criminologists called "the deep end" of the juvenile justice system. Instead, the superintendent of the institution established its internal rules, which included deciding when to release inmates who were serving indeterminate sentences. The autonomous nature of these institutions was especially troubling since so many juvenile reformatories were in reality miniprisons for minors. Mack's own attempt in 1907 to extend his court's jurisdiction over privately run Catholic institutions in Illinois had ended his brief but brilliant career as a juvenile court judge. Now, forty-five years later, Judge Bernstein was challenging the authority of the superintendent of the Arizona Industrial School for Boys.

Charles Bernstein personified Mack's Progressive Era vision of an ideal juvenile court judge. Born in St. Louis in 1904, Bernstein moved as an infant with his family to Los Angeles, received his LL.B. from Southwestern University in Los Angeles in 1929, married Blanche Friedman, the daughter of a prominent Phoenix family, and moved to the Grand Canyon State. He served as its assistant attorney general from 1937 to 1939, emerged as a leader in the state's Democratic Party in the 1940s, and in 1949 Governor Dan Garvey appointed him to serve on the Maricopa County Superior Court. Bernstein had become the first Jewish judge in Arizona. In addition to being a talented lawyer and respected jurist, he was exceptionally well versed in the professional literature on juvenile delinquency and law reform. According to leading authorities on delinquency in post–World War II America, adolescents, like adults, often suffered from psychological problems and could be "readjusted," except for those who were truly psychotic. Moreover, it was the responsibility of juvenile courts to provide clinical treatment, not corporal punishment. Thus, Bernstein enlisted psychologists and psychiatrists to work with the troubled youth brought to his court. He also prohibited his probation and detention officers from striking the wards of the court. Bernstein promised to have officers who violated this rule arrested and charged with aggravated assault.

Bernstein's role in investigating the Fort Grant scandal earned him national recognition in the field of juvenile justice. Later, he cemented his reputation as a children's advocate with his May 5, 1954, ruling in *Heard v. Davis,* declaring that the segregation of African American children in Phoenix's Wilson Elementary School District violated the equal protection clause of the Fourteenth Amendment to the U.S. Constitution. The U.S. Supreme Court, which was then preparing its landmark decision in *Brown v. Board of Education,* requested a copy of his opinion. Twelve days later, Chief Justice Earl Warren famously proclaimed that "separate educational facilities are inherently unequal."

Bernstein's accomplishments, such as his success in lowering the juvenile delinquency rate in Phoenix, helped him to win election to the Arizona Supreme Court in 1958. He spent ten years on the state's high court, serving twice as its chief justice. Significantly, in 1965, Justice Bernstein wrote the Arizona Supreme Court's decision in the case about due process in juvenile court that the U.S. Supreme Court reviewed in *In re Gault.*

Given the judge's background and reputation, it is not surprising that Phillip Pierce, one of the two seventeen-year-old boys featured in the *Time* article, sought out Judge Bernstein. The judge had worked closely with Pierce for several years and helped him to find shelter and employment. Pierce, who was still on probation in 1951, had left the state and stolen a car to go joyriding with friends in Needles, California. After Pierce was returned to Arizona, Judge Bernstein ordered a psychiatric exam. The doctor concluded that Pierce, an exceptionally good-looking white teenager with a near-genius IQ of 139, had become mentally disturbed when his mother had told him that she did not know who his father was. She called her fourteen-year-old son a "bastard." At that moment, according to the psychiatrist, Pierce began to lose his self-respect, gradually becoming angrier and angrier at society. The psychiatrist recommended twenty-four-hour supervision until Pierce's psychological issues could be resolved. He predicted that Pierce would eventually be able to enter the military. Since Fort Grant was the only secure facility in the state, on June 27, 1951, Judge Bernstein committed Pierce to the custody of George Ridgway, the new superintendent of the industrial school. Ridgway, a businessman and educator from nearby Safford, promised that he would work with Pierce to ensure that the boy could enlist in the Navy after his release.

Bernstein, who sent boys to Fort Grant only as a last resort, knew that the isolated industrial school, located on the lower slope of Mount Graham in eastern Arizona, was a harsh place. The Board of Directors of State Institutions for Juveniles, whose five members were appointed by the governor, was supposedly responsible for overseeing juvenile placements and parole in Arizona but was largely ineffective. Until the establishment of the Arizona Department of Corrections in 1968, the state's juvenile institutions operated autonomously. This allowed superintendents to create their own rules, but Bernstein expected that Ridgway, who had visited him in Phoenix after accepting the job, would run the industrial school humanely.

In 1950, before Ridgway became superintendent, the Superior Court Judges' Association of Arizona and the Board of Directors of State Institutions for Juveniles commissioned John Schapps and Milton Rector, the Western director and a field consultant for the National Probation and Parole Association, to study Fort Grant. The judges and board members were concerned about the number of boys who ran away from the school and how many of its graduates were incarcerated in the state penitentiary. Fort Grant, they believed, should be preparing its students for enlistment in the armed services, not criminal careers. The judges and board members wanted answers to two questions: "What's wrong at Fort Grant?" and "What should be done about it?"

Fort Grant, initially called Camp Grant, had a troubled history. Following the "Camp Grant Massacre" of 1872 in which a vigilante force of Anglo Americans, Mexican Americans, and Tohono O'odham Indians had murdered more than 100 sleeping Apache women and children outside the military base, the U.S. Army renamed the camp and relocated it to Mount Graham. More than 100 of the perpetrators were tried in Tucson. The trial lasted five days. After deliberating for only nineteen minutes, the jury found them all not guilty. The army relocated the remaining Apaches to the San Carlos Reservation.

In 1912, the U.S. government gave Fort Grant to Arizona, when the territory became the nation's forty-eighth state. Although the Arizona legislature had initially considered saving the costs of running a reformatory by shipping the state's juvenile delinquents to California for incarceration, lawmakers ultimately decided to use the fort instead. They liked that it was so far from either a railroad or a population center.

In the late 1930s, Arizona stopped housing girls at the school. From the 1940s to 1972, the state sent female delinquents to private facilities such as the Florence Crittenden Home and the Convent for Good Shepherd. Meanwhile, Fort Grant developed a reputation for brutality, becoming known to Arizonians as "desert Devil's Island." Over the years, several superintendents were fired because they tortured inmates.

Schapps and Rector were not the first investigators hired to study Fort Grant, but they hoped to be the last. In their report, they hammered home the idea that the industrial school had no place in the modern world of juvenile corrections:

> Old and isolated, Fort Grant, Arizona, U.S.A. occupies a tract of desert land on the lower slope of Mount Graham, 35 miles north of Wilcox, and 40 miles southwest of Safford. Here is situated the Arizona State Industrial School. No public carrier reaches the Fort; mail arrives three times a week; the School shares a multiple party telephone line with most of the neighboring ranches. Adobe buildings, designed and arranged as befitted a military post in the Indian country of bygone days still stand to house both staff and boys. The cavalry parade grounds and the walks and lawns are now bordered by trees grown large in the long years of decay and creeping obsolescence which have overtaken this ancient place.

Their detailed report provided a glimpse into daily life at the industrial school, including profiling its staff of thirty-three people. Superintendent Dr. E. L. Edmondson, who had earned his Ph.D. in Public School Administration from Northwestern University in 1940 and an honorary degree in medical science from Southern University in 1945, was in charge. His staff worked to maintain the decrepit facilities; supervised the preparation of meals, the laundry, the dairy, and the junior cottage and senior dormitory; managed other assorted work details; and directed the band and athletics. There were three full-time teachers but no mental-health professionals. The staff and their families lived on the grounds.

The investigators paid close attention to how children arrived at Fort Grant, more than a four-hour drive from Phoenix and accessible only via an unpaved road. For children in distant parts of Arizona, a sheriff or deputy had to drive them several hundred miles before delivering them, their commitment orders, and a record of their physical examinations to the school's dean of boys. Rarely did the school receive a boy's case record upon his admission, so school officials knew almost nothing about their newest residents.

New arrivals had only a vague idea about the school. The dean provided a new admit with a copy of the rules and regulations and a receipt for personal items. He took the boy to the barber and then to the laundry for a blue shirt, blue denim pants, and two pairs of shoes. The dean assigned him to a room. After a conference with the superintendent, administrative director, and foreman, the dean assigned the boy to a work detail. The new inmate then began working immediately.

This quick process contradicted the individualized casework approach that was the hallmark of progressive juvenile justice. As Schapps and Rector explained, "A diabetic lad should receive his medication regularly; a non-reader should have special help; a boy partly trained to be a plumber's helper . . . should be afforded the right job opportunities at the School; a boy unready for group life or to protect himself from sexual or other exploitation should rate a single room, not as a privilege, but as prescription in his special case." Their last example was one of many allusions to a culture of inmate violence that included fighting, rape, and occasionally suicide.

On June 1, 1950, the day that Schapps and Rector began their investigation, the school had only 77 inmates. This number was deceptively low because the industrial school averaged 125 inmates, and by the late 1950s it routinely held more than 250. Almost all the inmates present on June 1 were U.S. citizens, more than half came from the poorest sections of Phoenix and Tucson, and the remaining ones were from the state's rural areas. Two thirds of the inmates were "Latin Americans" (i.e., of Mexican ancestry) and Catholics, a half-dozen were Native Americans, another half-dozen were "Negroes," and the remaining handful were "Anglo Americans." The youngest inmate was nine years old, and there were three seventeen-year-olds. The majority were between the ages of twelve and sixteen years and enrolled in sixth, seventh, or eighth grade. Some boys had spent more than two years at the industrial school, most had been there for fewer than twelve months, and several had done time at Fort Grant before.

According to Schapps and Rector, the inmates ate ranch-style cowboy cooking, with beans as a staple "because of the Mexican boys." Although the boys were fed well and allowed to talk during meals, they were not well dressed. During the day, they wore their allotted blue shirts and pants. At night, even during the coldest months, they were permitted to sleep only in their underwear.

The older boys lived in a senior dormitory, often with three or four sharing a room designed as a single. The overcrowding was due to a shortage of space but was also rooted in the belief that putting more than two boys together in a room helped eliminate "sex play." The younger boys slept on bunk beds in a crowded junior cottage.

Arizona juvenile court judges had committed most of the boys for property crimes (twenty-nine for theft, nineteen for burglary, six for grand larceny), many for status offenses (five for incorrigibility, four for being involved in sex, three for truancy, three for running away from home), several for crimes against persons (three for assault, one for robbery), a few for dependency (two for growing up in a "dependent and inadequate home," one for being neglected), and one for an "unknown" reason.

The industrial school followed a regimented daily schedule, with only minor adjustments on weekends and holidays. The routine emphasized work and discipline for the older boys. During the school year, they received half a day of schooling during the week, before or after reporting to their work details. The younger children were enrolled full-time in school. Neither the older nor younger inmates attended Sunday school or participated in religious instruction, but a clergyman frequently showed inspirational films for Thursday's movie night.

Revealingly, forty-seven of the seventy-seven boys whom Schapps and Rector studied had tried to run away at least once from Fort Grant. Although they risked dehydration crossing the desert and faced severe punishment if caught, including whippings, they kept trying to escape. The school used bloodhounds to track down runaways and usually captured them within a couple of days. Schapps and Rector recommended that the administration work harder to "reduce the [boys'] urge and need to run away" and cautioned against enclosing the fort in a fence. As they noted, "Concentration camp fences surrounding training schools properties are not only inefficient barriers but psychological stimulants to 'escape plans.'"

Overall, it was a damning report. Schapps and Rector stressed that "LACK OF SUFFICIENT FUNDS, BAD LOCATION AND PHYSICAL PLANT, INADEQUATE AND UNDERPAID STAFF, LIMITED PROGRAM AND SERVICES, AND THE NEED FOR INCREASED PUBLIC UNDERSTANDING AND SUPPORT, ARE THE REAL PROBLEMS TO

BE FOUND AT FORT GRANT, AND WHICH UNDERLIE MOST OF THE DIFFICULTIES WHICH HAVE FOR YEARS INVOLVED THE BOYS, THE PERSONNEL, AND THE ADMINISTRATION." They urged Arizona to close down Fort Grant and replace it with a modern facility in either Phoenix or Tucson. The legislature rejected their recommendation.

Judge Bernstein, who had read Schapps and Rector's report and later visited the industrial school in May 1951, knew that Fort Grant had problems. Bernstein, however, was stunned to learn from Phillip Pierce that Ridgway and his staff were whipping the boys with fan belts and thick ropes, beating them with blackjacks, and forcing runaways to march barefoot more than thirty miles in the desert. He pulled "his kids" from the school, launched his own investigation, reported the allegations to the press, and ultimately filed contempt charges against the superintendent and his staff members.

Once the scandal became national news, including a story broadcast by NBC and an impending FBI investigation, the Arizona legislature established a Joint Committee to Investigate the Management and Operation of the Arizona Industrial School. Beginning in January 1952, a six-member committee chaired by State Senator William Kimball, a future senate majority leader and candidate for governor, conducted its hearings at Fort Grant and the Arizona State Capitol in Phoenix. They investigated the allegations by eighteen boys, including Phillip Pierce, and heard testimony from juvenile court judges, the inmates at Fort Grant, the staff, and state board members.

Seven of Arizona's fourteen juvenile court judges testified before the committee. The committee explained to the judges that it was conducting the hearings much like a juvenile court session and told the witnesses that their testimony would remain confidential. The legislature later reneged on this promise and published the transcript of the hearings. This valuable source serves as a window into the workings of post–World War II juvenile justice. It reveals contrasting visions of juvenile justice, such as disagreements among the judges on the appropriateness of corporal punishment and what constituted cruel and unusual punishment. Their reflections on which boys belonged at the school, and how they should be treated, demonstrate how protean the meaning of juvenile justice can be. The elasticity of the concept helps to explain why so many states and nations so readily embraced the idea of juvenile court. Communities, especially those that elected their own judges, could make these courts into a reflection of their values about childhood, proper parenting, and reasonable punishment.

The committee invited Judge Benjamin Blake, a member of the Church of Jesus Christ of Latter Day Saints, who had served as the superior court judge in Graham County since the early 1940s, to deliver the opening testimony. Fort Grant was located in Graham County, and the boys from the school had initially told their story of abuse to Judge Blake. The judge had told them, in no uncertain terms, that they got what they deserved. Blake stressed to the committee that Ridgway, who he thought was a Methodist, did not belong to his church. Blake had read accusations that he was "taking up for Ridgway" only to defend his own Mormon community.

Judge Blake articulated a desert vision of punitive juvenile justice that reflected Arizona's Southwestern political culture. The state fused traditional Southern values, brought to the region by nineteenth-century Southerners who settled the territory, with a frontier appreciation of rugged individualism and an accompanying distrust of government. As the criminologist Mona Lynch has noted, "This orientation in part accounts for the state's second-class treatment of minorities and the poor, in that the traditionalist culture promoted racial and class hierarchies, and the self-sufficient libertarian streak ensured little support for those who might need government assistance."

Blake believed that parents, not the state, were responsible for raising their children to be responsible citizens. This included whipping them. If a boy got into trouble, then Judge Blake held an informal hearing. As he testified, "It has been my purpose to call in the parents and only the parents. We don't have lawyers. My lawyers in my county have been very respectful. In some instances they have appeared as a friend and not as any attorney, and we simply try to make a fair diagnosis of that problem." The problem, as he explained, was whether the father was willing to straighten out his son. If so, then the judge put the boy on probation. In these cases, he believed that the boy would not return to court.

Questioning the judge's authority was not a good idea. As Blake noted, some parents complained that their sons had gotten a raw deal. Those boys, according to Blake, were likely to get into more trouble. After their third or fourth appearance in court, Blake sent them to Fort Grant. As he explained, "There is nothing that hurts me, no class of my work hurts me any worse than to send a boy or girl to the school, but I have done it when

I have been defied the third or fourth time, where there is nothing else left to do and still let them know that I am judge of the court."

The judge also strongly believed that the school needed to be able to discipline boys severely. According to him, 80 percent of the boys did well at the school, but the remaining 20 percent were troublemakers. The boys who had run away, he believed, belonged to the class of troublemakers. He noted, "I would say [Mr. Ridgway] disciplined them severely, but I think they needed it and it had to be done to maintain this school. Otherwise, I think Mr. Ridgway or anybody else might just as well step out and say, 'All right, you fellows take charge of your school.' That is my honest opinion."

Members of the committee and other witnesses, including the superintendent and his staff, expressed similar views about the importance of corporal punishment and blamed lax parenting for delinquency. For example, Judge J. Mercer Johnson of Pima County testified thus:

One of you members mentioned a minute ago about whippings on kids. I will say generally that the kids that I have sent up there probably didn't get any discipline at home. That was one of the reasons they are in the trouble that they do get into. I think maybe if their parents had exercised a little more supervision over them while they were at home, chances are they wouldn't be in the type of trouble that they are.

Judge Johnson explained that "Spanish-American" families were largely responsible for the problem of juvenile delinquency.

The majority of the kids that we send up there or that I send up there come from Spanish-American families. They lack so many facilities at home that you and I have or that our kids have that you can't wonder that they get into trouble. They have absolutely no supervision in many, many cases. They invariably come from the class of families that are in low financial conditions. Their housing conditions are bad. Many times when a kid has got in trouble so many different times I wouldn't have sent him to Fort Grant had he had the proper facilities at home.

He added,

As a matter of fact, when I send a boy up there, I tell him almost invariably that the reason he is going up there is because he hasn't had any discipline at home and I feel that by sending him there he is going to have the proper discipline and maybe when he comes out he is going to realize that he has to obey the law and abide by the same regulations that the rest of us do.

As his testimony reveals, the judge easily lapsed into the language of *us* and *them*.

Significantly, the supporters of corporal punishment used their private experiences as fathers who had whipped their own children to justify it. The following testimony, by one of the staff members accused of abusing the boys, highlights this form of argument.

I am an employee here, Terence J. Quinn. I am the one that administered a lot of the whippings. I have seen a boy hurt from his whippings. I wouldn't attempt to hurt a boy any more than I would attempt to hurt my little baby here, but she needs a whipping now and then and she gets it. I have been accused of being a big bruiser and a drunkard and a lot of other things, but I am not. I will take a drink when I am off duty. I may go so far as to say I will have several. At Christmas time, I had a few eggnogs, things like that. But I am not a big bruiser. I was whipped about as many times when I went to school as I have been since. A lot of these boys right on our grounds out here could whip me, but I don't fight with them. When they need disciplining, I take them in the office. They are disciplined. Some of them do scream, but I don't believe it is unjust. My baby will scream, too, sometimes before I get the razor strap off of the hook, but most of the time she minds. These boys are beginning to mind. It has taken quite a little while. I think I have worked for George Ridgway now for about seven months, and he is a very good boss.

The deep end of juvenile justice—as described by Terence J. Quinn—was a culturally different place than Judge Bernstein's modern, psychologically informed courtroom in Phoenix.

The proponents of corporal punishment supported it in the context of a separate justice system for juveniles. Ridgway, for example, argued that even the most disobedient boys should be treated as juvenile offenders, not transferred to the state penitentiary. When the chairman of the committee asked Ridgway whether judges should have committed the most serious offenders to Fort Grant or the penitentiary, Ridgway supported keeping them in the juvenile justice system. He stated, "I had hope for them, but—I would hate to condemn any boy. I still say I had hopes. I hope I could, but I doubt that I could do any good. But I don't condemn a boy. I don't call the third strike on him at all. I never have and will never do it."

Desert juvenile justice thus emphasized discipline and control while simultaneously embracing the principle of diverting children from the adult criminal justice system. To justify corporal punishment, its proponents drew on the common-law notion of *in loco parentis* ("in the place of a parent") to analogize the superintendent and his staff to parents and teachers who, under Arizona law, could physically punish children. Corporal punishment was considered reasonable punishment for children and youth, but Arizona prohibited its use in the State Penitentiary, which housed mostly adult felons.

The experience of World War II, as it turned out, forced several juvenile court judges to reevaluate the limits of appropriate discipline. Judge Don T. Udall of Navajo County, for example, drew on his own experiences as a lieutenant colonel in the Judge Advocate General's Corps to argue forcefully that any disciplinary practices that the military banned, such as forced marches in bare feet, were cruel and unusual punishments that had to cease. A number of the other judges noted that Udall's thoughts on this subject had influenced them.

Judge Bernstein adamantly opposed any form of corporal punishment for older children and teenagers. As he testified,

> My dad used to paddle me when I was a little guy and I think maybe it helps little fellows, but after a boy gets older and larger, that isn't going to help at all as to his hostility, and if you permit any form of corporal punishment, it is a matter of progressive brutality. It is ten paddles this time and fifteen the next and then thirty and then there is no stopping.

Instead, Bernstein stressed his faith in a therapeutic role for the state. He told the committee this:

> I think that this juvenile program for kids in this state is a disgrace for the state of Arizona. We are paying them money for it; we are entitled to the services. We are entitled to see that these kids are properly treated. They are maladjusted, disturbed boys. They wouldn't be there

if they were not. The whipping of them is not going to change them, because they been whipped and roughed at home, and the idea of saying that they should have been whipped a long time ago is an absurdity. Most of them have been, and beaten badly, by their parents trying to drill something into them, but that didn't work.

He added, "Each one of these kids has to be worked upon on an individual basis with a good study, a study of the social background, and a medical study, his physical defects, if any, psychological and psychiatric. Then that officer working with these kids will know the kid's individual problem and try to meet it and try to help me." This professional discourse of juvenile justice placed faith in mental-health experts to diagnose and adjust boys who did not conform to societal norms.

In response to Bernstein's argument for a psychologically informed approach to juvenile justice, Representative David G. Watkins remarked, "Well, it would seem to me that under your theory Ridgway might be able to do a good job if he had a staff of trained psychiatrists." Bernstein instead suggested that the legislature reconsider Schapps and Rector's report on Fort Grant, which had called for replacing Fort Grant with a modern training school in one of Arizona's two major cities, so that the school could work with mental-health experts already in the community. He also recommended that Arizona follow California's lead in adopting the American Law Institute's model legislation for establishing a youth authority that substituted rehabilitation for retribution as the overriding mission of juvenile corrections. John Ellington, the executive secretary of the American Law Institute, who had led the successful campaign for the law's adoption in California, had recently visited Judge Bernstein's chambers to discuss the theory and practice of this new approach to juvenile corrections. Bernstein recommended that the committee members invite Ellington to testify, but they did not.

Judge Bernstein, the advocate for individualized treatment, and Representative Julliette Willis, a staunch defender of the desert vision of punitive juvenile justice, clashed repeatedly. Citing her experience as a mother, Willis questioned that idea that juvenile delinquents, including those at Fort Grant, required individualized treatment.

Rep. Willis: But Judge, the Army has one set of rules for everybody that comes into the Army. The Navy has one set of rules for everybody that comes into the Navy. I will admit that you have to have a certain intelligence before you can get in, but most schools have one set of rules for everybody that goes to that school. Why do we have to be different at Fort Grant? It seems to me, well, you can say, well, they are potential criminals and they will be a cost to the state, so therefore we ought to do more for them than we do for our own boys who don't go to Fort Grant. I am a mother. I have a nineteen year old boy. I have seen a lot of boys around my house. I have seen a lot of different types. I have three or four nephews. I have had some that have been in trouble. But they all had to abide by the same rules in the family.

Judge Bernstein: We are talking about a different thing, though. We are talking about the disturbed boy, the maladjusted boy, the boy that is not conforming.

Rep. Willis: Well, I have seen mine disturbed at times, too, and he certainly conformed.

Judge Bernstein: We are not talking about that type of disturbance, Mrs. Willis, not at all.

Simply put, Judge Bernstein and Representative Willis worked from different assumptions and spoke different languages.

Judge Bernstein, the strongest supporter of modern juvenile justice practices, was also the jurist who made the strongest case for transferring boys from the juvenile court to the adult criminal justice system. Bernstein explained that Arizona law granted juvenile courts original and exclusive jurisdiction over the cases of all people younger than eighteen years old. This meant their cases had to begin in juvenile court. He pointed out, "But [the law] doesn't say that they are not capable of violating the law. We know that they are, and they can be just as vicious and violate just as many laws as adults. But a juvenile court is not a punitive court, it is a court of readjustment and rehabilitation, and the court is charged with that responsibility." He added,

There is no place in this set-up for jailers for boys. If these boys are so bad that they can't be handled fair, then they should be placed in the penitentiary. They should be referred to the adult court for that purpose, and that is what the law provides if they are that type, because we are charged not only with doing what is [in] the best interest of the minor, but we are charged with the protection of society.

Since the opening of the first juvenile courts in the early twentieth century, judges had transferred a small percentage of cases to the adult criminal court system, often those of adolescents near the upper age limit of the court's jurisdiction.

After hearing testimony from the juvenile court judges, the committee invited the boys who alleged that they had been abused, beginning with Phillip Pierce, to tell their stories. Pierce, who had been released from Fort Grant on January 4, explained that he had immediately sought out Judge Bernstein. "I thought maybe he would do something that would help the boys that are up there and are going to be there. A lot of kids get beat for things that they don't even do a lot of times. A lot of times the guards are drunk and they just come in and beat you for general principles." At the prompting of the committee, Pierce named names. He reported which staff members drank on the job; those who kicked, punched, and used blackjacks on the boys; and why he and two other boys had tried to escape from Fort Grant in September. He also described what happened after they were caught, such as being forced to march barefoot across the desert.

Representative Willis asked Pierce, "How did you happen to get your discharge, just because you served the length of time?" He replied, "I was a good boy." "You are a good boy?" she responded incredulously. "Yes. I was making A's. Four months after we came back from running away I got discharged." Willis then wanted to know what he thought about the other inmates, and what kinds of boys he thought should be sent to the school. "Don't you think if he steals, or anything that a grown person ...," she asked before Pierce interrupted her. He stated, "There's three kids you are going to talk to, Augustine Tisnado, Jimmy Acevez, and Mitchell Thomas. Mitchell Thomas has got twenty people living in his family, and Tojo, he hasn't got nobody to go to, and Jimmy is his half brother, he hasn't got nobody to go to. He has been up there five years now. Do you think that is right?" Willis asked, "What did he go up there for?" Pierce answered, "Because he didn't have any place to go." Chairman Kimball immediately ended this line of questioning.

Pierce and the other boys singled out Rudolph "Rudy" Ramirez as the most abusive staffer but were reluctant to criticize Superintendent Ridgway. Pierce pointed out that when he went to see Judge Bernstein, he did not want to get Ridgway in trouble because "he is a nice man, you know, but people are running over him." According to Pierce, the real problem was too many of the staff were "bachelors and they don't know a kid from anything." Willis used this statement as an opening to discredit Judge Bernstein by again invoking parenthood as a form of expertise. She asked Pierce, "Do you think that people that have children understand children better than people that don't have children?" "Yes," he replied. "Judge Bernstein doesn't have children. Do you think he understands them?" Pierce answered, "He has made a study of it." At this point, Chairman Kimball tried to bring the session to a close.

He thanked Pierce for his testimony and asked if he had any final thoughts for the committee. Pierce shared his assessment of what was wrong with the officers at Fort Grant who did not "understand kids." Either they were bachelors "or they've got kids and they've got wives that boss them around so they will take it out on the kids." He elaborated, "I mean, this guy from Kingman used to be Rudy's house boy and he used to go home every afternoon—he'd go over there and clean up the house, and he said he could hear Rudy's wife bawling him out all the time, so every time she'd bawl him out he would get drunk and come out there and beat the hell out somebody." Willis quipped, "Well, maybe bachelors are better than married men, then. They don't have wives to bawl them out." Pierce responded, "No. I don't know, people tell me that it is supposed to be an industrial school to learn things, and the ones that are bachelors up there think it is a prison." "Do you think you learned anything up there?" Willis asked. "Yes," Pierce replied. Willis added, "You learned that you didn't want to go back." This time she had the last word.

The testimony of the other older boys followed a similar pattern, with the committee members asking to hear their own stories and then cross-examining them. They also asked each witness to describe the other boys at the institution, especially those who had made the most serious allegations.

The staff members questioned by the committee denied the worst charges, like drinking on the job and beating the boys with blackjacks. Although the committee had promised the boys that their testimony was confidential, members read accusations from the transcript to the staff and told the officers which boys had made the statements. A committee member would then ask the witness whether the statement was true or false. The officers acknowledged using fan belts to whip the boys and forcing them to march barefoot across the desert but disputed the length of these forced marches. Shortly before Rudy Ramirez testified, he resigned. He denied that anyone had forced him to do so and that he had done anything wrong during his time at the school.

Several members of the Board of Directors of the State Institutions for Juveniles, including Chairman Louis Felix, testified. Felix was furious that Judge Bernstein had spoken to the press about the allegations. He believed that Bernstein had hurt Arizona's reputation and that the judge was attempting to seize control of the industrial school.

> These outrageous charges were broadcast in the newspapers, they were broadcast over the National Broadcasting Company. The former Mayor of Tucson, Joe Niemann, told me he was in San Francisco the night that it was flashed out over the air, and he said it just sounded very, very bad for the state of Arizona as a whole and it was very injurious publicity and I think something that is going to take a long time to live down.

Moreover, he was frustrated. "So this Board now feels, where do we stand? Who has the authority and where does the authority come from and how far does it go? We felt we were in charge of the School or, at least, until we were proven inefficient. Now the judiciary department seemingly has taken over. They are calling our staff out to come to Prescott and Phoenix."

Bernstein's contempt case against Ridgway was the elephant in the hearing room. Yavapai County juvenile court judge W. E. Patterson had also filed contempt of court charges against the superintendent and his staff. During his testimony before the committee, Ridgway asked Chairman Kimball for help, but Kimball explained the he could not give him legal advice. Ridgway replied, "Well, I've got to find somebody to give it to me."

Fortunately for Ridgway, two old friends took his case. Richard "Dick" Chambers, who had grown up in Safford, graduated from Stanford Law School, and now had a successful law practice in Tucson, agreed to help his childhood friend. Jesse A. Udall, a lawyer in Safford, also agreed to represent him. Chambers and Udall later became influential jurists— Chambers served as the chief judge of the United States Court of Appeals for the Ninth Circuit and Udall served as the chief justice of the Arizona Supreme Court.

Their legal strategy rested on asking the Arizona Supreme Court to halt the contempt trial on procedural grounds. If the state then decided to file criminal charges against him, Ridgway would at least benefit from having a jury trial. In a contempt trial, as in a juvenile court hearing, a judge decided the defendant's fate. The burden of proof and rules for presenting evidence in a contempt case were also less demanding than in a criminal trial. Chambers, who considered the charges against Ridgway "nonsense," was offended by how Judge Bernstein and Judge Patterson had skirted around the criminal law. He later explained to the Arizona historian and author of *The Banana Farm*, Hal Herbert, that "two Superior Court Judges cited him for contempt of court on unfounded charges, to be tried by themselves or someone of their choice without a jury far from home." Chambers objected to the judges treating Ridgway, in effect, like a juvenile delinquent.

Their legal argument was elegant. Once a minor was committed to the State Industrial School, the judge had remanded custody to Arizona's executive branch. If the state's juvenile court judges were allowed to instruct the superintendent about how to run the school, then the superintendent would be forced to serve "fourteen masters"—a reference to the Gospel of Matthew's injunction, "No man can serve two masters." The judicial branch would be running a department of the executive branch, which was a clear violation of separation of powers. The problem was that an Arizona Supreme Court decision from 1925, *Howard v. State*, held that superior courts had continuing jurisdiction "to proceed by contempt for violation of their orders." Thus, Chambers and Udall were asking the Arizona Supreme Court to overrule settled law on constitutional grounds.

On June 9, 1952, in *Ridgway v. Superior Court of Yavapai County*, the Arizona Supreme Court agreed that the contempt trial violated separation of powers, halted the proceedings, and overturned its earlier ruling in *Howard*. The *Ridgway* decision emphasized the primacy of the legal process over the outcome in a particular case. Justice Arthur La Prade's opinion mirrored the Cold War context of the early 1950s, when Americans defined their system of government as the antithesis of either Nazi Germany or Stalinist Russia. Legal-process theorists, for example, stressed the importance of the proper governmental institution making decisions and worked to delineate the proper role for courts in a democratic society. "Our philosophy and legal approach to the concept of governmental theory under which we live suggests to us," La Prade stated, "that the judiciary should closely scrutinize its assigned field or sphere and rotate in its own orbit. The courts are not the masters nor are they vested with totalitarian powers to correct all evils and aggressions on the rights of our citizens." He added,

> That they are solicitous of the welfare of our people is to be expected and commended, but under our scheme of government there are other branches manned by officers of like attitudes and sensibilities to whom is assigned the duty of governing such institutions as the one under review. In so doing they have prescribed powers and duties all of which have been enacted and promulgated by the people, speaking through the legislative branch of the government.

In other words, Judge Bernstein and Patterson had flown outside of their proper orbit. Similarly expressed concerns about judges exceeding their authority became commonplace in the wake of the Warren Court's controversial decisions in the 1950s and 1960s, such as *Brown v. Board of Education* and *Miranda v. Arizona*.

Unlike Ridgway's attorneys, who played down what had happened to the inmates of Fort Grant, Justice La Prade, a former Phoenix district attorney and state attorney general, emphasized that the justices "do not want it understood that this court condones in the slightest the more serious specifications set forth in the several rules to show cause. If the assaults charged were in fact committed their perpetrators should be prosecuted, but the short-cut route selected was without authority of law." In a dissenting opinion, Justice Marlin Phelps contended that his colleagues had misconstrued the Arizona Constitution and the relevant statutes. He believed that the superior court had the authority under Arizona law to determine "whether the officials or employees of the industrial school have overstepped the rules of propriety or committed any wrong whatsoever." Phelps believed that the contempt trial should proceed, but he was the lone dissenter.

The *Ridgway* decision meant that juvenile court judges in Arizona no longer had any control over what happened to the children and adolescents they sent into the deep end of the state's juvenile justice system. Furthermore, on October 7, 1955, the Arizona attorney general affirmed in published opinion no. 55-202 that the superintendent of Arizona Industrial School could constitutionally administer corporal punishment to an inmate of that institution so long as "it does not verge on willful inhumanity or oppression." Consequently, criminal charges were never filed against George Ridgway and his staff.

In 1953, Steve Vukcevich, a politically connected rural Democrat, replaced Ridgway and fired the remaining employees who had been charged with contempt of court. He also eliminated the forced barefoot marches. According to *History of Fort Grant, 1872–1972*, six months later, Governor Howard Pyle proclaimed that Fort Grant was now "a sanctuary for boys not a desert devil's island." Until 1973, when the state converted Fort Grant into an adult prison, Vukcevich ran it as a military academy. The boys wore uniforms, had to participate in drills, and followed a strict code of conduct. As a proponent of the desert vision of punitive juvenile justice, Vukcevich emphasized discipline over rehabilitation. He hired no mental-health professionals until well into the 1960s. He also retained a modified version of Ridgway's corporal punishment policy until 1969, when the newly created Department of Corrections banned whipping juvenile inmates with a razor strap.

The Arizona Industrial School for Boys never had another scandal like the one that Phillip Pierce and Judge Charles Bernstein exposed. Fort Grant, however, continued to make the desert vision of punitive juvenile justice into a living reality for its inmates, including two boys whose names have been inscribed in American constitutional law: Ernesto Miranda (committed in 1956) and Gerald Gault (committed in 1964).

CHAPTER 2

"Do You Have Big Bombers?"

In 1960 the Gault family (Paul and Margaret and their sons Louis and Gerald) became part of the great Southwestern migration that altered the nation's demographics and transformed American politics, culture, and law after World War II. The Pennsylvania family loaded their car and headed west for the promised land of southern California. A similar car trip in 1946 by the songwriter Bobby Troup and his then-wife, Cynthia, had inspired the lyrics for "(Get Your Kicks On) Route 66," first recorded and popularized by Nat King Cole that same year. The song that celebrates freedom in the age of the automobile concludes in San Bernardino. The Gaults, however, never made it to the Golden State. Their car broke down ninety miles east of Phoenix, and they could not afford to have it repaired.

The Gaults had become the newest residents of Globe, Arizona. 6,217 people lived in the copper-mining and mill town that served as the seat of government for Gila County. Noted Arizona essayist and environmentalist Edward Abbey described Globe as "one of Arizona's most important smog producers," located in the "good desert country, of the lower Sonoran zone, rich in giant cactus, such as the saguaro, and unusual wildlife, such as the javelina." The javelina is "a small piglike animal that never weighs over fifty pounds. Almost half the bulk of this creature is taken up by the head, so that it looks like a caricature of a pig, as a child might draw one." In the early 1960s, the Globe Chamber of Commerce launched the Javelina Derby, an annual event that awarded prizes to hunters for killing these animals, with separate awards for bow and gun hunters.

A century earlier, miners had discovered silver in this part of the Arizona Territory and later founded Globe in 1876. The town was located in the foothills of the Pinal Mountains, about 3,500 feet above sea level, just west of the San Carlos Apache Reservation. During the 1870s, U.S.

troops and Native American tribes waged the Apache Wars in the region. Hostilities ended in September 1886 when Geronimo, the famous Chiricahua warrior, surrendered to General Nelson Miles in nearby Skeleton Canyon.

During the 1880s, Globe's economy shifted from silver mining to copper production and the prosperous town soon played an important part in Arizona history. George Wylley Paul Hunt, who had run away from home in 1878 to explore the West, arrived in Globe three years later. He worked for a decade as a miner and rancher before taking a job as a delivery boy for the town's general store. The store merged with the Old Dominion Commercial Company, and Hunt eventually became president of the successful company. He then decided to enter politics. In 1893, he won election to the Arizona Territorial Assembly. Known as the "Old Walrus," Hunt was five-feet-nine and bald, wore a handlebar mustache, and weighed almost 300 pounds. He became the territory's most recognizable and outspoken political figure.

In 1910, Hunt served as the president of the Arizona Constitutional Convention. When Arizona became a state in 1912, he was elected its first governor. He served seven two-year terms and championed progressive causes such as woman suffrage, compulsory education, child labor laws, old-age pensions, and workers' compensation laws. During World War I, he worked as a federal labor arbitrator for the Wilson Administration. After the war, he served as the U.S. minister to Siam for a year before returning to Arizona. He was the state's governor for much of the 1920s and won his final term in office in 1931.

In 1960 Globe still resembled the scenic town the Old Walrus had called home. Its prominent downtown buildings had been built during the early twentieth century, including the four-story Gila County Courthouse, the Gila Bank and Trust Building—designed by Chicago architect Louis Sullivan—and the Alden Theatre, an Art Deco and Spanish colonial structure. The town's train depot, its most luxurious hotel, the Old Dominion, and its elegant Globe Theatre were also built during the Progressive Era. The lack of air conditioning in the Globe public schools made life for children growing up in the 1960s similar to the experiences of past generations. Middle school–aged children also attended Central School, which had been built in 1891 and enlarged with an addition in 1912. It was the oldest operating school building in Arizona.

Globe, whose population was declining, embodied Arizona's past, not its future. The state itself was experiencing a population explosion. From 1950 to 2000, it was the second-fastest-growing state in the nation. The Pentagon's decision during World War II to establish air force bases and pilot training fields in Arizona had attracted corporations such as Goodyear, Alcoa, and Motorola to build plants nearby and transformed the state. And the influx of Republican Midwesterners to Phoenix restructured politics in the Grand Canyon State. It would no longer be run as a traditional one-party state controlled by the Democrats. The 1952 Senate race reflected this changing political landscape. Republican Barry Goldwater, who later became the national face of modern conservatism, triumphed over Democrat and U.S. Senate Majority Leader Ernest McFarland. The urban Republicans championed economic development and modernizing state government. A significant but smaller number of liberal Democrats who moved to the Tucson area also supported these changes.

To modernize the state's government and economy, the Arizona bar and bench called for amending the state's 1912 constitution. The constitution reflected Progressive Era concerns about the power of judges. It provided for only a limited state judicial system and allowed for the popular recall of judges. President William Howard Taft, a former federal judge himself and later the first president to become chief justice of the United States, angrily vetoed the initial resolution for Arizona statehood because he opposed this judicial recall provision. The state had to remove it before Taft would approve Arizona statehood. After achieving statehood, the people of Arizona restored the recall provision to their constitution. They also punished Taft in the 1912 general election. He finished fourth in the state's popular vote—behind even the Socialist candidate, Eugene Debs.

In 1960 Jesse A. Udall, who had successfully defended George Ridgway during the Fort Grant scandal, now campaigned for Proposition 101—the Modern Courts Amendment—a state ballot initiative to replace the judicial article of the state constitution. Udall, who had recently become a justice on the Arizona Supreme Court, argued that this change would allow for reorganization of the state judicial system to improve its efficiency and to standardize courtroom procedure. In a luncheon address to Sertoma Service Club of Mesa, Udall explained,

> Like Moses and the Drafters of Magna Carta, we are faced with an archaic system that was adopted back in "horse and buggy days" when

the state was sparsely populated. It goes without saying, that to meet the requirements of our present day, with vast changes in every field of endeavor, we must be awake to our responsibilities and make our constitution fit the requirements of 1960.

Otherwise, he warned, Arizona courts would be unable to keep up with their heavy caseloads. "Justice delayed," he cautioned, "is oftentimes justice denied." Such delays also impeded economic development.

To garner support for the Modern Courts Amendment in Tucson, the Pima County Bar Association invited U.S. Supreme Court Associate Justice William O. Douglas to deliver an address. A member of the court since 1939, Douglas was a westerner who oversaw the Ninth Judicial Circuit, which included Arizona. He also lived in Arizona during part of the year. As Douglas stated, "a man's rights may be greatly depreciated if he must wait two or more years to get inside a courtroom to establish them. It is a hopeful sign that the issue of delay in Arizona's courts is being met with a boldness and determination that is characteristic of the West." At heart, Douglas was a legal realist who cared more about practical results than pure reasoning. In his address, he underscored the importance of having excellent people serve on the bench. "There is indeed," he declared, "hardly any problem of judicial administration—apart from the sheer volume of cases—which cannot be answered by high quality judges." Fortunately, he concluded, the Modern Courts Amendment would allow Arizona to "construct the framework of a workable system under which able and conscientious judges will thrive and dispense justice with even hands."

On November 8, 1960, Arizonans approved the Modern Courts Amendment, which refined the jurisdiction of the state's superior courts. This included giving these courts "exclusive original jurisdiction in all proceedings and matters affecting dependent, neglected, incorrigible or delinquent children, or children accused of crime, under the age of eighteen years." This meant that the superior court initially heard all cases involving children under the age of eighteen. "The judges shall," according to Arizona law, "hold examinations in chambers for all such children concerning whom proceedings are brought, in advance of any criminal prosecution of such children, and may, in their discretion, suspend criminal prosecution of such children." Thus, after hearing a juvenile case, a judge could determine that the child should be prosecuted in the adult criminal justice system. Finally, the amended constitution concluded, "The powers of the judge to control such children shall be provided by law."

Gerald "Jerry" Gault, who was only eleven years old when the Modern Court Amendment passed, probably knew nothing about it. As a transplanted Pennsylvania boy in strange new surroundings in the Southwest, he most likely cared more about the World Series, especially since a team from his home state was playing. The memorable series ended when Pittsburgh Pirates second baseman Bill Mazeroski homered in the bottom of the ninth inning of game seven to defeat the heavily favored New York Yankees.

The national pastime, as it turned out, landed Jerry in trouble with the law for the first time. On Monday, July 2, 1962, Jerry, now thirteen, was accused of stealing a baseball mitt. The Globe Police Department referred his case to the Gila County Juvenile Court. Counties in Arizona with fewer than 30,000 people, such as Gila County, had only one juvenile court judge. A probation officer investigated the incident and decided that Judge Robert E. McGhee did not need to hold a hearing on the matter. Like many children, Jerry had his case informally "adjusted" by the intake staff member in the probation department at the front end of the juvenile justice system. The probation officer concluded that the boy's family could handle their child. Since no official record of this first encounter with the juvenile court was kept, whether Jerry had done anything wrong is unclear.

Jerry stayed out of trouble for eighteen months. His family moved to Globe Mobile Homes, a trailer park. His father worked on construction projects in New Mexico and later the Grand Canyon. His mother worked as a babysitter in a childcare center, and his older brother, Lewis, had also begun working.

The year 1964 did not turn out well for Jerry. His problems began on Sunday, February 2, 1964, when Mary Hernandez had her wallet stolen from her purse in the Alden Theatre. It contained $60. Witnesses reported seeing several boys leaving the movie theatre, and the police questioned Jerry. He told the police officers that he had seen Curtis Uptain steal the wallet and had followed him out of the theatre. With Jerry's help, the officers located Curtis. Both boys were charged with grand theft, referred to the juvenile court, and detained. At 11:15 P.M., the police notified both boys' parents of their arrest.

The next day, Curtis Uptain was scheduled to appear before Judge

McGhee. McGhee, who was born in Idaho in 1914, had moved as a young boy with his family to Douglas, Arizona, located near the Mexican border. He graduated from the University of Arizona in 1939, enrolled in the university's law school, but interrupted his studies to serve for five years in the U.S. Army during World War II. Afterward, he completed his law degree and was admitted to the bar in 1947. He moved to Globe, served as city attorney, and in 1959 won election to the Gila County Superior Court. He was the fourth superior court judge in the county's history and remained on the bench until 1975. Thus, for sixteen years Judge McGhee determined what juvenile justice meant in Gila County.

McGhee, a proponent of the desert vision of punitive juvenile justice, committed eleven-year-old Curtis Uptain to the Arizona Industrial School for Boys on an indeterminate sentence. Unless Superintendent Steve Vukcevich released him, Curtis would remain incarcerated at Fort Grant until he reached his twenty-first birthday on November 28, 1973. Stealing $60 had potentially cost the fifth grader close to a decade at Fort Grant, although most first offenders were released after only six months. Gila County juvenile justice could be swift and severe.

In Jerry Gault's case, it was slower and gentler. At the end of the week, the chief probation officer filed a delinquency petition against Jerry. Deputy Probation Officer Charles Flagg conducted the investigation into the boy's life and interrogated Jerry for more than three hours. He recommended placing the boy on six months probation. Judge McGhee signed the probation order that instructed the eighth grader to "stay out of trouble" and "obey your mother."

While Curtis Uptain was adjusting to life at Fort Grant and Jerry Gault was completing his probation, Judge McGhee and Chief Probation Officer Ralph Henderson traveled to Tucson in May for a continuing-education program staged by the National Council of Juvenile Court Judges. The theme of the conference was "the Juvenile Court as an Agent of Change." McGhee and Henderson listened to "a brief theory lecture" on "Levin's Force Field Analytic approach to the induction of change," brainstormed about the dilemmas their court faced, broke into small groups to learn about the dynamics of involvement/non-involvement in group decision-making, and watched thirty-eight minutes of the film *12 Angry Men*. They had to predict the order in which the jurors would shift their votes from "guilty" to "not guilty." The conference ended with a ninety-minute session devoted to translating "the workshop learnings into back-home application." But it would take more than one conference to transform Arizona's juvenile courts into agents of change. A summary report, prepared by Dr. Jay Hall, the director of the Southwest Center Delinquency and Youth Problems Project at the University of Texas, noted that "the judges were generally reticent." He added, "Perhaps a longer period of the same type of training would prove more effective with this group in the future." He was, however, optimistic. "In general," he concluded, "the session seemed to go well and may have some long-term effects once the incubation period characteristically following a training experience has had time to run its course."

Back in Globe, Jerry Gault had stayed out of trouble and was close to completing his probation. On Monday morning, June 8, 1964, he was home alone. His father was out of town working on a project at the Grand Canyon, his mother was babysitting, and his brother was at work. His friend Ronnie Lewis came over around ten. Ronnie said that his father wanted him to call and arrange for Ora Cook to clean their trailer. Since Lewis's home had no phone, Ronnie's father had sent him to use the Gaults'. To ensure that Ronald did not make an expensive long-distance call, Jerry insisted on dialing the five-digit number. What happened next is unclear, except for the following events. One or both of the boys made sexually suggestive overtures to Cook, Ronnie left, Cook called the police, and the police traced the call to the Gault phone. A few minutes later, Officer Trojanovich arrested Jerry at home and then found and arrested Ronnie. The boys were charged with making "lewd phone calls" and locked in the Gila County Jail's "drunk tank." The police officer referred their cases to the juvenile court.

Once more, Probation Officer Flagg was assigned a case involving Gerald Gault. He interviewed Jerry, who said that Ronnie had said all the dirty words over the phone. In his brief report, Flagg scribbled: "Gerald says Ronnie ask (this woman today) 'Are your cherries ripe? Do you have big bombers? Do you give any away? Do you have a big long prick?'" Although Jerry did not admit to saying any dirty words, Flagg found it incriminating that Jerry had memorized Cook's phone number. Surprisingly, Flagg did not interview Cook in person. Instead, he telephoned her to discuss the obscene phone call.

Margaret "Marjorie" Gault returned home at 6:00 P.M. with her son Louis and was surprised that Jerry was not home. She began to make dinner and sent Louis to find Jerry, who they assumed was at the Lewis's family trailer. Louis learned that Jerry and Ronnie had been arrested, so Marjorie went to the Detention Home to find him. Officer Flagg, who filed the delinquency petition against Jerry, told her that she could not see him that evening and that the juvenile court would hold a hearing in his case "tomorrow, about 3:00 o'clock."

The next afternoon Judge McGhee held the initial hearing on Jerry's case in his chambers. Six people were present: the judge, probation officers Flagg and Henderson, and Jerry, Louis, and Marjorie Gault. No one recorded what was said during the informal hearing. Later, during a habeas corpus hearing on August 17, Marjorie Gault, Judge McGhee, and Probation Officer Flagg provided different accounts of how Jerry had answered the judge's questions. Marjorie Gault testified Jerry told the judge that he dialed the number and asked the woman whether she was Mrs. Cook. He stated, "There is a friend of mine here wants to talk to you," and then handed the phone to Ronnie. Ronnie, not Jerry, then uttered the dirty words. Jerry's mother had not heard her son confess any wrongdoing.

Judge McGhee remembered the hearing differently. He testified that Jerry had admitted making "silly calls, or funny calls, or something like that" with his brother before the family had moved to Arizona. According to the judge, Jerry also admitted that he had "said some lewd words." Officer Flagg also testified that Jerry had admitted making at least one of the lewd statements.

The judge also said that they discussed the boy's school work and home life. McGhee recalled

> some talk about him wanting to go to—the Grand Canyon with his father. He said that if his father hadn't let him down—his father had promised to take him to the Grand Canyon, but then when it came time to go, he just went off and left him; and he cried, he said, well, if—if his dad had just taken him to the Grand Canyon, this would all never have happened.

McGhee also emphasized that they spent much of the initial hearing discussing Jerry's previous trouble with the law. The judge testified,

> We also talked—there was quite a discussion at the time about his previous times in court, and I remember specifically telling him that, "You remember when you were here before I told you what might happen if you would get into trouble." There was some discussion that—on

other occasions he had been falsely accused. All these other charges he had been somewhat falsely accused, except the one in February he did admit being involved in this.

Although the participants offered strikingly different accounts of the hearing on June 9, all agreed on its outcome. The judge decided that he needed more time to think about the case. He remembered telling the Gaults, "I am going to think it over and—and let you know something about it in the future." In the meantime, Jerry remained in custody.

The next day, June 10, Jerry's father learned that his son was in trouble. He had called his wife from the Grand Canyon. After learning the news, he headed back to Globe. Jerry was released to his mother's custody on Friday, June 12. At 5:00 P.M. that evening Officer Flagg delivered a note to the family, stating only "Mrs. Gault: Judge McGhee has set Monday June 15, 1964 at 11:00 A.M. as the date and time for further Hearings on Jerry's delinquency." Around midnight, Paul Gault returned home.

On Saturday, the anxious parents spoke with Rob Weinberger, who was their landlord and the Chief of Police. They asked him if they needed a lawyer. Weinberger told them it was not necessary. "Judge McGhee," he said, "was giving the boy a year's probation." The relieved parents decided not to retain counsel.

Lawyers rarely appeared in juvenile cases to either prosecute or represent a child. Judge Paul W. Alexander of the Toledo Juvenile Court, for example, said, "We seldom see a lawyer in juvenile court—and when we do, we have to tell him what to do and how to do it." John J. Molloy, who served as the juvenile court judge in Tucson, agreed with this characterization. He added, "It is my opinion, that, on the whole, practicing lawyers did their clients as much harm as good when appearing for them in the juvenile court." Tellingly, Molloy explained, "It may be well that the opinion I happen to hold in this matter is a very erroneous one. I find myself in the position of being unable to defend it within the confines of any strictly legalistic discussion." Instead, he used the concerns about "the extent of family disunity and juvenile delinquency" to justify the informal juvenile court process in Arizona and elsewhere.

Jerry's second hearing included more participants than the initial hearing. This time Ronnie Lewis and his father attended. Jerry's father was also there. Ora Cook, however, was not at the hearing. Once again, no one was sworn in and no transcript was produced. At its conclusion, McGhee ruled that Jerry should be sent immediately to Fort Grant to serve an in-determinate sentence. This amounted to a potential six-year prison sen-tence for allegedly making a lewd phone call. Under Arizona law, if Jerry had been an adult, he could have been sentenced to no more than sixty days in jail and ordered to pay a $50 fine. The judge's ruling stunned Jerry and his family. They had expected probation, not prison.

Marjorie Gault's questioning of Judge McGhee during the second hearing may have sealed Jerry's fate. She had asked why Mrs. Cook was not in court to identify which boy "spoke dirty to her." Judge McGee said that Cook did not need to be present and apparently was offended by the tone of Mrs. Gault's inquiry. Before Jerry was taken away, Marjorie asked permission to kiss her son goodbye. Jerry had never spent a night away from home. The judge refused her request. He told her that "she ought to be sent down to Fort Grant."

Once incarcerated, Jerry learned one lesson in the deep end of juvenile justice. A couple of weeks after Jerry's arrival, a boy who had cerebral palsy hanged himself after being raped. To survive, Jerry decided, he had better become the meanest kid there.

Meanwhile, Paul and Marjorie Gault searched for a lawyer to help them get their son back. They travelled to Phoenix and met with Philip Haggerty, a young attorney who served as the chief criminal trial law-yer in the Arizona attorney general's office. Haggerty referred them to Amelia Lewis, a much more experienced lawyer and transplanted New Yorker. Lewis, who was born in the Bronx in 1903, graduated from St. Law-rence Law School (now Brooklyn Law School) and became one of the few women admitted to the New York bar in the 1920s. She practiced law in New York City for thirty-three years, was actively involved in the Ameri-can Civil Liberties Union, raised three sons, and moved to Arizona after her husband died in 1957. She passed the Arizona Bar Examination in 1958 and opened her own law practice in Sun City, a retirement community outside of Phoenix.

On August 1, 1964, six weeks after Jerry had been sent to Fort Grant, Paul and Marjorie Gault met Lewis. As a mother who had raised three boys, she was horrified by what had happened to Jerry and agreed to take the case. Lewis first assumed that they could appeal Judge McGhee's rul-ing but learned that Arizona barred appeals in juvenile court cases. Her only option was to file a habeas corpus petition. A habeas corpus hearing focuses on the legality of the process by which the individual has been detained, not his or her innocence or guilt. For centuries English and American jurists, including Sir William Blackstone and Chief Justice John Marshall, had considered habeas corpus the "great writ of liberty." If a judge determined that a person was being held illegally, the court would order immediate release of the prisoner.

On August 3, Lewis met with Justice Lorna Lockwood of the Arizona Supreme Court to discuss filing a habeas corpus petition. Born in Douglas, Arizona, in 1903, Lockwood was the same age as Lewis. Her father had served on the Arizona Supreme Court and perhaps more importantly had introduced his daughter to Sarah Herring Sorin. In 1902, Sorin had become the first woman admitted to the Arizona bar. She practiced mining law in Globe and became the twenty-fifth woman to argue a case before the U.S. Supreme Court. Sorin inspired Lorna Lockwood to become a lawyer.

Lockwood graduated from the University of Arizona and in 1925 became the first woman to graduate from the university's law school. Due to gender discrimination, she had difficulties finding work as a lawyer and spent fourteen years as a legal stenographer and secretary. She then formed the first all-woman law practice in the state. In 1939, she was elected to the Arizona House of Representatives and then worked as the district price attorney for the Office of Price Administration during World War II. After the war, she returned to the state legislature. In 1949, she became the first woman to serve as assistant attorney general for Arizona. Two years later, she became the first woman trial judge in the state. She served for ten years on the Maricopa County Superior Court and presided over its juvenile department from 1954 to 1957.

As a juvenile court judge in Phoenix, Lockwood continued the progressive approach that Charles Bernstein had popularized. She stressed that the juvenile court "has a two-fold purpose—to protect human rights and to enforce human responsibility." Like Bernstein, she was also concerned about the conditions of confinement. After inspecting the county juvenile detention center, she ordered two iron cells welded shut because no child should be held in them. She also organized the Arizona Conference on Crime and Delinquency Prevention and Control and helped found the Arizona Chapter of Big Brothers and Big Sisters, as well as a residential treatment center for delinquent girls.

In the 1960s, Lockwood continued her pioneering legal career. In 1961, she was first woman elected to the Arizona Supreme Court. Four years later, she became the first woman in American history to become chief justice of a state supreme court. In 1967, President Lyndon Johnson considered nominating her to become the first woman justice of the U.S. Supreme Court. Johnson instead selected Thurgood Marshall, who became the first African American justice.

When she met with Justice Lockwood on August 3, Lewis had not yet prepared a formal habeas corpus petition but showed her Paul Gault's affidavit. It stated, "Deponent is advised by his attorney and therefore believes that his said son is being detained from his parents unlawfully; that his commitment was illegal." The judge, according to the affidavit, based his finding of delinquency "on insufficient evidence" and had advised neither Jerry nor his parents of their right to counsel. In addition, the process was flawed because "no testimony was taken," the parents did not know what their son had been charged with, and the victim did not testify. Thus, the court had deprived the parents of their right to the custody of their son. After reading the affidavit, Lockwood told Lewis to add only a caption and that she would accept the "petition in the form of affidavit." She then called the chief judge of the Maricopa County Superior Court to arrange for a superior court judge to hold a habeas corpus hearing.

Lockwood may have also read Marjorie Gault's affidavit but did not cite it in her order for the habeas corpus hearing. The mother's affidavit provided more information about the facts of the case, such as Judge McGhee telling Marjorie that she belonged in Fort Grant. Her affidavit concluded, "Petitioner has consulted with an attorney of the Arizona Civil Liberties Union now and believes that there is not sufficient [evidence] to show her child to be delinquent; she has not found him anything than an obedient boy who has gotten into some trouble, not of a serious enough nature for the punishment meted out to him." In short, Marjorie thought that her son's punishment was unreasonable.

Significantly, two accomplished women lawyers had initiated an ancient legal process that could potentially free a modern adolescent who may have been imprisoned not for what he allegedly said over the telephone but for what his mother had said to a juvenile court judge. By August 17, the date set for the habeas corpus hearing, Jerry had already spent more than sixty days at Fort Grant—the maximum sentence he could have received if he were an adult convicted of making an obscene phone call.

Maricopa County Superior Judge Fred Hyder presided over the day-long habeas corpus hearing. He succinctly defined his role. "If I must find there was jurisdiction, your habeas corpus would fail. . . . If there was no jurisdiction, you must prevail." Judge Hyder insisted that both parties stipulate that they would "not go into the evidence as to the boy's guilt of a crime." The hearing was thus supposed to focus only on the legitimacy of the legal process, not Jerry's innocence or guilt. Amelia Lewis represented the petitioners (Paul and Marjorie Gault), Attorney General Robert W. Pickrell and Assistant Attorney General Philip Haggerty represented the respondent (Superintendent Vukcevich), and a court reporter transcribed the proceedings. Jerry was present, but neither side called him as a witness to testify because the hearing focused on the jurisdiction of the juvenile court and the parental rights of Paul and Marjorie Gault. In this legal setting, Jerry was expected to be seen, not heard.

Lewis contended that Paul and Marjorie Gault's parental rights had been violated because the state had not followed due process in taking Jerry away from them. Haggerty, who conducted the direct examination and cross-examination for the state, argued that due process had been followed. The parents, he insisted, had known that the case involved the obscene phone call and understood their right to call witnesses and retain an attorney.

Lewis called only Paul and Marjorie Gault to testify. Through their testimony, she showed that they had never received notice of the specific charges against their son or been told of their right to retain counsel or call witnesses. Haggerty's cross-examination revealed that the parents knew that the case was about an obscene phone call to Ora Cook and that they had chosen not to exercise their rights.

Although both parties had agreed not to address the evidence about Jerry's innocence or guilt, Haggerty made sure that his two witnesses testified that the boy was guilty. On the stand, both Deputy Probation Officer Charles Flagg and Judge Robert McGhee stated that Jerry had confessed to saying at least one of the obscene words during the initial hearing. Flagg also testified that Ronnie at his own initial juvenile hearing had accused Jerry of using obscene language over the phone. Ronnie, unlike Jerry, never had a second hearing. His family sent him out of state to live with relatives in California.

Judge McGhee's testimony was the most revealing and contentious part of the day. Lewis objected to Haggerty's asking McGhee questions about what Jerry had said at the hearing because this line of questioning was immaterial. The real issue, she stressed, was whether the first and second hearings had followed due process. Judge Hyder overruled her objection. Consequently, Judge McGhee testified that Jerry had confessed at both hearings. The judge recalled that during the initial hearing,

> He admitted at that time that he had said some lewd words. It was concerning sex, and if I remember right, the one he had, would she give him a little; but there was some other—other words about "Have you got big bombers," or things like that. I don't remember exactly which one it was, but he admitted making one of those. But he accused the other boy of doing most of the talking.

The judge also stated that during the second hearing, Jerry had made "some admission again of some of the lewd statements."

During her cross-examination, Lewis questioned the judge about the legitimacy of the initial hearing. As the judge explained,

> I consider it a hearing, yes. The parent was there, and the boy was—a statement was made as to what it was about, and what the probable consequences were of a boy getting into trouble; and I don't know—I don't know, I don't believe that the statute requires a written notice. It's been my practice that if they do appear voluntarily for the hearing, and we proceed with it, it's a hearing.

His description captured the informality of a juvenile court hearing in a small town like Globe.

Since the process was so informal and there was no appellate review of juvenile court cases, Judge McGhee was not accustomed to explaining his decision-making. He had a difficult time, for example, articulating how he applied the relevant laws or why he had sent Jerry to Fort Grant. Lewis began with a straightforward question. "Now, Judge, would you tell me under what section of, of the code you found the boy delinquent?" He replied,

> Well, there is a—I think it amounts to disturbing the peace. I can't give you the section, but I can tell you the law, that when one person uses lewd language in the presence of another person, that it can amount to—and I consider that when a person makes it over the phone, that it is considered in the presence, I might be wrong, that is one section. The other section upon which I consider the boy delinquent is Section 8–201, Subsection (d), habitually involved in immoral practice.

Thus, according to McGhee, Jerry had violated two different laws. The judge, however, emphasized the language in the juvenile code about being habitually immoral. Lewis then asked, "Judge, would you tell us the immoral matters in which he was involved in that led you to the decision?" He replied, "Yes. Yes, I can tell you that. On July—let's see. On July the 2nd, 1962, there was a referral made to our office. Thought it was not—a referral was made, no follow-up was requested by the Globe Police Department, where the boy had stolen a baseball glove from another boy and lied to the Police Department about it. Also. . . ." Lewis interrupted, "Excuse me, was there a hearing held in your Court on this matter?" McGhee answered, "There was no hearing. No hearing." Lewis asked, "There was no accusation, then?" McGhee said, "There was no accusation."

Lewis then asked the judge about the specific language of the juvenile code that addressed vulgar and obscene language. McGhee stated, "I consider it an immoral matter when a boy calls some—a lady up on the telephone and ask [sic] her to give him a little, and talks about the bombers, and that sort of thing. I consider that immoral in connection with Section 8–201, Section D." His use of the personal pronoun "I" speaks volumes about the power and discretion of a juvenile court judge. Under Arizona law, he had no need to specify why a child was delinquent or explain his reasoning to anyone.

When Lewis asked him about "the additional bases, if any, upon which you found him 'habitually immoral,'" Judge Hyder interrupted. He asked, "Aren't we going outside the issues of the case here, Mrs. Lewis?" Lewis replied, "Well, this is a—actually the first time in which I am learning something about the case, Judge. This is the first time I am learning that the boy was considered habitually immoral." Judge Hyder stopped this line of questioning. As he explained, "If there was jurisdiction, then it's not up for this court to determine whether or not the Court of Gila County acted with wisdom or whether or not this Court would act the same." The habeas corpus hearing was, of course, not supposed to address innocence or guilt.

Much as the doctrine of separation of powers had protected the executive branch from judicial oversight in the Fort Grant scandal in 1952, the circumscribed nature of the habeas corpus hearing prevented Judge Hyder from reviewing McGhee's discretionary judgments. Just as the superintendent of the industrial school could autonomously run his institution, a juvenile court judge had autocratic control over the administration of justice in his or her court. Thus, the internal workings of both the front and deep ends of the Arizona juvenile justice system were largely insulated from external judicial review.

In addition to stopping Lewis from questioning McGhee about why he found Jerry delinquent, Judge Hyder also ordered that "the testimony of Judge McGhee, with respect to finding the child delinquent under Section D be stricken for the fact that there is nothing in the record of the Juvenile Case which shows that he was found delinquent under Section D, 8–201." Lewis asked that his testimony remain in the record. This part of Judge McGhee's testimony would play an important role in the U.S. Supreme Court's *In re Gault* decision.

The habeas corpus hearing revealed the discretionary nature of juvenile justice. Parents like Paul and Marjorie Gault never received the specific charges against their children in writing. An exchange between Lewis and McGhee drove this point home. Lewis asked, "Did your Honor at any time apprise the parents of the exact charges against the boy, citing the sections of the law that you say he had violated?" Judge McGhee replied, "No, it's not the practice to cite the sections of the law because the—the law says that you only—you do not set out in your petition the facts, merely that the boy is delinquent. That's all the law requires."

At the conclusion of the hearing, Judge Hyder delivered his ruling in one sentence. "It is ordered, adjudged and decreed that the petition be dismissed and the Writ discharged and that Gerald Francis Gault be remanded to the custody of the respondent." This meant that Jerry was going back to Fort Grant. Unlike a juvenile court decision that could not be appealed, the order of a judge in a habeas corpus hearing could be appealed directly to the Arizona Supreme Court. Thus, Amelia Lewis had another chance to gain Jerry's release.

With the financial and legal support of the Arizona Chapter of the American Civil Liberties Union, Lewis petitioned the state supreme court on November 17, 1964, to review not only Judge McGhee's handling of the case and Judge Hyder's ruling, but also the constitutionality of Arizona's juvenile court law. She asked the justices to "take a second look at the Juvenile Code of Arizona and how the children of this state are faring under it, to the end that just and consistent procedures be established." Her request for fairness and consistency sounded similar to the arguments of the state's bar and bench in their 1960 campaign for the adoption of the Modern Courts Amendment.

The Arizona Supreme Court accepted the case. Their review of the case occurred during an especially fluid period in the history of due process and habeas corpus. Beginning in 1961 with *Mapp v. Ohio,* the U.S. Supreme Court launched a due process revolution that extended protections in the Bill of Rights to people in state criminal courts. In *Mapp,* the Supreme Court applied the Fourth Amendment's exclusionary rule (i.e., judges should exclude from criminal trials evidence obtained illegally) to the states. The following year, the court used *Robinson v. California* to apply the Eighth Amendment's ban on cruel and unusual punishments to the states. And, in 1963, the court delivered its famous *Gideon v. Wainwright* decision, which extended the Sixth Amendment right to assistance of counsel to state defendants in felony cases. That same year, in *Fay v. Noia* and *Townsend v. Sain,* the court lowered the procedural hurdles for state defendants petitioning for habeas corpus hearings in the federal courts.

To keep up with these dramatic changes in case law, in 1963 Chief Justice Charles Bernstein and Vice Chief Justice Lorna Lockwood organized a two-day conference on judicial proceedings. They invited Justice Roger Traynor of the California Supreme Court, one of the most respected and influential state jurists of the twentieth century, to lead sessions on the latest developments in criminal procedure, such as the exclusionary rule and the right of indigents to counsel. The state superior court judges attended the workshop and the *Arizona Weekly Gazette* printed and distributed the booklet to judges and lawyers. Thus, the Arizona Supreme Court helped educate the state bar and bench about what now constituted due process across the nation.

The U.S. Supreme Court, however, had never decided a juvenile justice case. Several years earlier, the justices had rejected a petition for certiorari (a request to review) regarding *In re Joseph Holmes,* a 1954 Pennsylvania Supreme Court decision. The petitioners had asked the high court to hear the case to answer three constitutional questions.

1. Does the due process clause of the Fourteenth Amendment apply to juvenile court proceedings?
2. May a State, consistent with the equal protection clause of the Fourteenth Amendment, deprive juveniles in juvenile court proceedings of protections which are available to adults in both civil and criminal litigation?
3. To what extent does the Fourteenth Amendment limit a State's

power to deprive children of their liberty as a result of juvenile court proceedings which are based on the sociological theory that children are the wards of the States?

By declining to hear *Holmes,* the justices left these questions unanswered.

This was about to change. On June 22, 1964—exactly one week after Jerry Gault had been committed to Fort Grant—Chief Justice Earl Warren delivered an address, "Equal Justice for Juveniles," to the Annual Conference of Juvenile Court Judges at the Shoreham Hotel in Washington, D.C. Warren discussed the international debate over the proper function of juvenile courts.

> In one camp are those who maintain that the juvenile court, as a court of law, must surround the juvenile with all the legal processes which would be available to him were he tried as an adult. The opposing view is that the social, emotional, educational, health and economic needs are paramount and the task of the court is to meet these requirements without concerning itself too greatly with legal niceties.

Warren could not say how he would rule on issues that might come before his court, but he reminded the judges that they were "lawyers first of all and pledged to follow the statutes under which you operate and, of course, to observe basic constitutional rights."

Although he did not specify what those constitutional rights were, he mentioned the legal issues involved in juvenile justice. For instance, he stated, "It would not be proper and I know that you would not wish me to say here whether I think, for instance, that every child brought before the court must be represented by counsel. That will have to wait until proper cases come before the court." He added, "I can say, however, that I think lawyers can be most useful and helpful to the court."

In a similar fashion, he spoke about evidentiary matters and due process requirements. "Nor can I say here whether strict rules of evidence must be followed," he stated, "but I can suggest that a reasonable adherence to orderly presentation of the facts in a particular case will prevent miscalculations and minimize the possibilities of miscarriages of justice." He elaborated, "To what extent the rules of criminal procedure applied in adult courts should be followed in juvenile courts is, as you know, a matter of controversy." Once again, he suggested his preference: "It does seem to me, however, that it is altogether possible to develop and draft practical, straight-forward, and understandable procedures applicable to juvenile courts."

In case the audience missed the implications of his address, the Chief Justice emphasized, "[W]e will come to grips and resolve finally such questions as to whether, as a matter of right, a juvenile delinquent is entitled to trial by jury, whether the privilege of confrontation, self-incrimination, proof beyond a reasonable doubt, admission to bail, and so on applies." He had clearly signaled that the Supreme Court was finally ready to hear cases that dealt with these issues.

The most striking feature of Warren's address was his emphasis on the idea that children had constitutional rights. He declared, "No boy or girl of whatever age can be permitted to run roughshod over the rights and property of others. He must be dealt with sternly but patiently, calmly, and understandably, mindful always of his rights as an *individual human being*." Warren admitted that this powerful idea that children had rights was a recent historical development, but emphasized that it was an idea that courts, including his own, could no longer ignore.

The U.S. Supreme Court was still searching for its first juvenile court case to review when the Arizona Supreme Court decided *In the Matter of the Application of Paul L. Gault and Marjorie Gault, father and mother of Gerald Francis Gault, a Minor, for a Writ of Habeas Corpus.* Chief Justice Lorna Lockwood assigned Charles Bernstein, the former Phoenix juvenile court judge who had made the Fort Grant scandal into national news, to write the court's opinion. On November 10, 1965, Bernstein filed the unanimous opinion for Lockwood, Jesse Udall, Ernest McFarland, Fred Struckmeyer, and himself.

By the time that the Arizona Supreme Court decided his parents' case, Jerry was no longer physically at Fort Grant, but he remained under the school's jurisdiction. He had spent 161 days at the desert's Devil Island before receiving a home placement.

Bernstein's fifteen-page opinion provided an exegesis of juvenile case law. In the process, Bernstein analyzed many of the same issues that Earl Warren had addressed in "Equal Justice for Juveniles." Like the chief justice, Bernstein highlighted the debate between proponents of traditional due process and those who favored a sociological approach to juvenile delinquency prevention and treatment. Bernstein, like Warren, emphasized that "the problem is ascertaining the particular elements which constitute due process in a juvenile hearing." Moreover, Bernstein also spoke about fairness for children, not only the rights of adults. "Good intentions do not justify depriving a child of due process of law.... Fairness is not inimical to the proper treatment of juveniles. Justice is as good for them as it is for adults."

Unlike Warren, who speculated about future cases, Bernstein had a specific one to review. "Our task," Bernstein explained, "is to determine the procedural due process elements to which an infant and his parents are entitled in a juvenile court hearing and decide whether our statute may be construed to include them. Then we must decide whether petitioners and their son were deprived of those rights to their prejudice." Bernstein's point of departure helps to explain his conclusions. He emphasized that the justices of the Arizona Supreme Court believed in judicial restraint. "We approach this challenge to the juvenile code," he noted, "aware of our duty to give to the language of all statutes a meaning that will render them constitutional if this can reasonably be done. We will not declare a legislative act unconstitutional unless satisfied beyond a reasonable doubt of its invalidity." He added, "In short, our duty is to reconcile the language of a statute with the constitutional provisions if possible."

Not surprisingly, Bernstein rejected all of Lewis's arguments that the Arizona juvenile code was unconstitutional on its face (i.e., the law itself, not its administration, violated either the Arizona or U.S. Constitution). For example, he dismissed Lewis's contention that the absence of appeals from juvenile court hearings violated the Arizona constitution. Instead, he reconciled the denial of appeals with the state constitution's granting superior courts "exclusive and original jurisdiction in all proceedings and matters affecting delinquent children." This minimalist approach prevented Bernstein from declaring the law itself to be unconstitutional, but there was a chance he would find that Judge McGhee had applied it improperly.

After noting that most appellate courts had not required "the full array of criminal procedural safeguards" in juvenile court, Bernstein examined the conflicts over "particular procedural safeguards." He parsed the case law, the Arizona constitution, and the relevant statutes to explicate the specific due process procedures that the state's juvenile court judges must follow. He concluded that a juvenile court had to provide written notice, although specific charges did not have to be listed. The court had to inform the child and his parents or guardians of the facts no later than the initial hearing. If the family denied the charges, then they had to be given a reasonable amount of time to prepare for the adjudicatory hearing. Also, although a judge could rely on hearsay evidence, "sworn testimony must be required of all witnesses including police officers, probation officers and others who are part of or officially related to the juvenile court structure." Finally, the judge had to determine whether evidence that a child had committed the alleged delinquency met the standard of being both clear and convincing. Thus, Bernstein and his colleagues agreed on the need for several procedural requirements.

On the other hand, Bernstein asserted that there was no right protecting juveniles from self-incrimination and that due process did not require that the parents have counsel. The court, however, could not deny them representation of their own choosing. Moreover, there was a right to confrontation of witnesses only if the charges were denied. Since there was no right to an appeal, he concluded there was also no right to a transcript because its purpose was largely "to support an appeal."

Bernstein concluded that Judge McGhee had followed these minimal procedural requirements. He pointed out that "Mrs. Gault knew the exact nature of the charge against Gerald from the day he was taken to the detention home. She and Gerald appeared at the first hearing without objection. Mr. and Mrs. Gault, together with Gerald, appeared at the second hearing before Judge McGhee without objection. Petitioners knew they could have retained counsel, called witnesses and cross examined Probation Officer Flagg." Thus, Bernstein argued, Judge McGhee had not denied Paul and Marjorie Gault's right to due process. Bernstein also concluded that Judge Hyder had properly conducted the habeas corpus hearing.

Since the Arizona juvenile code itself was constitutional and Judge McGhee had followed the minimal requirements for due process, Justice Bernstein concluded, "The Order of the Maricopa County Superior Court is in all respects affirmed." Jerry thus remained under the jurisdiction of the Arizona industrial school.

Amelia Lewis had lost in Arizona, but all was not lost. The next week she met with the Northern Arizona Chapter of the American Civil Liberties Union (ACLU) to get permission to appeal the case to the U.S. Supreme Court. She also wrote to Melvin Wulf, the National Legal Director of the ACLU, to seek the support of the National Board. Locally and nationally the ACLU assisted her in filing the appeal and drafting a jurisdictional statement. Lewis argued that this obscure case from Arizona raised federal constitutional questions that only the U.S. Supreme Court could decide. On March 8, 1966, she mailed Wulf the transcript of the habeas corpus hearing, the abstract of the record, and Justice Bernstein's opinion for the Arizona Supreme Court. She noted, "I will also send my draft of the jurisdictional statement and request that you take the matter from here. Your name will go on the case as you are admitted before the U.S. Supreme Court and I assume that you will argue the matter."

Thus, a case that began with a boy whose family had moved to the Southwest and then experienced desert juvenile justice would now be handled by a New York City lawyer representing the nation's leading civil liberties organization.

PART II

Legal Liberalism

CHAPTER 3

"It Is Going to Be a Great Case"

In 1962, Melvin Wulf became the national legal director of the American Civil Liberties Union (ACLU). It was the heyday of legal liberalism. Proponents of this philosophy believed that courts, especially the Supreme Court under Chief Justice Earl Warren, could be used as instruments to bring about meaningful social change nationwide for historically disadvantaged groups, such as African Americans, women, and children. Accordingly, the ACLU itself flourished during the 1960s. Its membership doubled to more than 100,000, local chapters formed in almost every state, and Wulf implemented its new legal strategy. Instead of primarily filing amicus curiae ("friend of the court") briefs in U.S. Supreme Court cases to alert the justices to specific issues, the ACLU would directly represent clients like Gerald Gault.

On March 16, 1966, Wulf invited Gertrude "Traute" Mainzer to work on the jurisdictional statement for *Gault*. The statement needed to demonstrate that the Supreme Court had jurisdiction to hear the appeal, and more importantly it had to convince the justices that the case presented a substantial federal question. Identifying and explicating the substantive constitutional issues raised by Jerry's case was the critical task at this stage of the litigation.

The lawyers who worked on *Gault* had to explain why this obscure Arizona case mattered for all the nation's children and youth subject to the jurisdiction of juvenile courts. Mainzer brought a unique perspective to the issues involved. She was born in Germany in 1914, survived a concentration camp, and later graduated from New York University law school after World War II. She worked as a research consultant for the Arthur Garfield Hays Civil Liberties Program at New York University's Law School. Founded in 1958, it was the only legal center in the United States that focused on civil liberties. Its director, staff, and law students worked closely with the ACLU, the National Association for the Advancement of Colored People, the Congress on Racial Equality, the American Jewish Congress, the Anti-Defamation League, and the Workers Defense League.

As Wulf explained to Mainzer, "I have not read the record as yet so I have no opinion on whether Mrs. Lewis' Statement of Facts is satisfactory. In any case, I suggest that you examine the record carefully to see whether you want to make any changes in the Statement of Facts." He added, "Though the section of the Statement explaining why the questions are substantial should be short, I am afraid that Mrs. Lewis took that suggestion much too literally. That section of the Statement needs some explanation. If you will send me a copy of your redraft when it is completed, we can all get together and go over it." After reviewing the case file, Mainzer told her boss and friend Norman Dorsen that *Gault* raised important constitutional questions, but they would have to rework Lewis's draft of the jurisdictional statement. They had until early May (about six weeks) to complete the assignment.

Dorsen, who became the Director of the Hays Program in 1961, was a rapidly rising star in constitutional law. Born in 1930, he had graduated from the Bronx High School of Science at age sixteen and then from Columbia College four years later. At Columbia, he had played on the varsity basketball team with Amelia Lewis's son, Frank. Dorsen next attended Harvard Law School and served as an editor of the *Harvard Law Review* (1951–1953). After graduating, he became a first lieutenant in the Judge Advocate Generals Corps of the United States Army. In that capacity, he assisted Special Counsel for the Army Joseph Welch during the famous, televised Army-McCarthy hearings in 1954. He then spent a year as a Fulbright scholar at the London School of Economics before beginning a clerkship with Associate Justice John Marshall Harlan of the U.S. Supreme Court.

His clerkship with Harlan, the grandson and namesake of the great dissenter in *The Civil Rights Cases* (1883) and *Plessy v. Ferguson* (1896), provided Dorsen with an insider's knowledge of the Supreme Court. It also cemented his reputation as a legal genius. Dorsen became friends with many of the justices, including William Brennan, who was emerging as a coalition-builder on the Warren Court. Many of the justices expected that Dorsen someday would argue a case before the high court.

After completing his clerkship, Dorsen returned to New York City to practice law. The election of John F. Kennedy in 1960 and his call for public service, "My fellow Americans: ask not what your country can do for you—ask what you can do for your country," encouraged Dorsen, like so many others, to contemplate a career in government. He applied for an appointment in the new administration, noting "my primary interest is a legal (or possibly administrative) job in the international field—State, U.N., economic aid programs, etc." Although Dorsen instead accepted a position at New York University Law School, he had many friends in the Kennedy and Johnson administrations. He advised then–Attorney General Robert Kennedy (the president's younger brother) on legal and political issues, worked on Kennedy's successful 1964 New York Senate campaign, and continued to work with the senator on policy matters.

The Kennedy Administration had inaugurated a new era for American juvenile justice. Robert Kennedy believed that the federal government should play a more central role in addressing the problem of juvenile delinquency that had attracted so much media attention during the 1950s. In May 1961, President Kennedy issued an executive order establishing the President's Committee on Juvenile Delinquency, to be chaired by his brother Robert. On the same day, the president sent to Congress the Juvenile Delinquency and Youth Offenses Control Act. In September, President Kennedy signed this landmark legislation that authorized $30 million for grants to support local delinquency-prevention projects. The United States Department of Health, Education and Welfare created the Office of Juvenile Delinquency to oversee the grants.

After months of interviewing experts on delinquency, Special Assistant to the Attorney General David Hackett arranged for Lloyd Ohlin, the research director of the Columbia University School of Social Work, to be appointed director of the Office of Juvenile Delinquency. Ohlin and Hackett developed and implemented delinquency prevention policies aiming at empowering local communities and minority youth. This community-based approach challenged the assumptions of the individually focused psychological explanations of juvenile delinquency that had been so popular since the 1940s. The Office of Juvenile Delinquency also sponsored many of the studies of juvenile courts in the 1960s that would inform the *Gault* litigation.

The pilot community programs in delinquency prevention established during the Kennedy administration also served as the launching pad for President Johnson's Great Society. Partly influenced by Michael

Harrington's *The Other America* (1962), which had exposed the extent and depth of poverty in the nation, Johnson's War on Poverty used the power and purse of the federal government to assist the disadvantaged. The administration introduced many innovative anti-poverty programs, such as Headstart, Jobs Corps, and Upward Bound.

The national focus on poverty and federal support of legal aid for the poor encouraged a new generation of lawyers, such as Dorsen and his colleague Charles Ares, to champion what was becoming known as "social welfare law." A transplanted Arizonan who had clerked for Supreme Court Justice William O. Douglas, Ares, like Dorsen, had joined the New York University faculty in 1961. Ares called for law schools to revamp their curriculum to address how the law could serve the needs of the poor. Typically, a bankruptcy course focused only on the interests of creditors, but Ares called on them to consider also the interests of debtors. But the expansion of the federal government since the New Deal to provide more social services also exposed an underlying tension in twentieth-century liberalism. As increasing numbers of Americans became entitled to the services of the welfare state, some liberals worried that governmental agencies and officials violated the constitutional rights of their clientele, such as their right to privacy. Social welfare thus appeared to be a new legal frontier.

This convergence of social welfare and civil liberties led Dorsen to create a Project on Social Welfare Law. He invited Ares to serve as a consultant. Dorsen also convinced Elizabeth "Wicky" Wickenden, a legendary pioneer in the field of social services and a politically connected Washington insider who had moved to New York City, to serve as a consultant. Wickenden's participation helped Dorsen further cultivate his connections to the Johnson administration as well as the Supreme Court. Once the project was established, Traute Mainzer became its research associate. It was in that capacity that Mainzer began to review the *Gault* case file.

It was fitting that *Gault* became a focus for the Project on Social Welfare Law. The juvenile court itself was an uneasy experiment in combining social welfare and crime control. The ACLU's decision in 1966 to litigate *Gault* exposed a generational rift among liberals. Roger Baldwin, who had founded the ACLU in 1920 and directed it for thirty years, had served as the first chief probation officer of the St. Louis Juvenile Court in 1908. With Bernard Flexner, the secretary of the National Probation

Association, Baldwin also had co-written the first textbook in the field, *Juvenile Courts and Probation* (1914). For them, what were most significant were the needs of poor children and their families, not formal due process. Baldwin, who was eighty-two years old when Gerald Gault's case reached the ACLU's offices, still believed in this benevolent vision of the juvenile court as a gateway to social services. He told his friend Dorsen, who was nearly a half-century younger, that the ACLU should not attack the juvenile court.

From the perspective of younger lawyers at the forefront of the 1960s due process revolution, the juvenile court was a suspect institution. For the *Columbia Law Review,* Ares favorably reviewed Margaret K. Rosenheim's *Justice for the Child* (1962), a collection of ten essays on the modern juvenile court, written by leading judges, lawyers, sociologists, and social workers. Ares noted that these experts represented a growing consensus that believed the juvenile court "has failed to live up to its promises. Indeed, there are strong reasons to believe that many of those promises were incapable of fulfillment." He highlighted the contribution of District of Columbia Juvenile Court Judge Orman Ketcham, who also served on the executive committee of the Advisory Council of Judges of the National Council on Crime and Delinquency. Ketcham, long a leading advocate of juvenile court reform, argued that unless states changed how they handled children's cases, then "the whole juvenile court experiment" would be "swept away by the tide of legal history." These necessary changes included providing "due process and fair treatment for the child and his parent" and appropriating the "sufficient funds for the prompt construction and adequate staffing of institutions truly designed to provide delinquent and dependent juveniles the care, guidance, and discipline that should have been provided by their parents." Building on Ketcham's analysis, Ares explained, "It is first of all necessary to recognize that, under the best of systems, the state when it acts through the juvenile court intervenes in a very drastic way in the lives of the child and his parents. No matter how benevolent the intent, the result is governmental coercion. For whenever the state does something for a child it also does something *to* him." Moreover, the "realities of the juvenile court system demonstrate that, while paternalistic and benevolent in design, the juvenile court in important respects is hardly different from the criminal court. Thus, it is being increasingly questioned whether traditional safeguards that protect the individual charged with crime should be altogether discarded in juvenile proceedings." Ares pointed out that New York and California had already revised their juvenile codes to provide for a right to counsel.

Ares worked on *Gault* briefly while at New York University before returning home to Arizona to serve as the dean of the University of Arizona's law school. Ares and Amelia Lewis continued to provide assistance from Arizona, but New York lawyers remained the driving force behind the case.

From the beginning Norman Dorsen considered *Gault* a logical follow-up to *Gideon v. Wainwright* (1963), the landmark U.S. Supreme Court decision that had guaranteed the right to counsel in all felony cases. The Supreme Court had appointed Abe Fortas, whom Anthony Lewis described in his 1964 bestseller *Gideon's Trumpet* as "a high-powered example of that high-powered species, the Washington lawyer," to represent the indigent Clarence Gideon. Dorsen had also played a vital role in the case. He worked with Melvin Wulf and former Attorney General J. Lee Rankin on the ACLU's amicus brief in *Gideon*. Dorsen was responsible for drafting a brief that was remarkable for its exhaustive analysis on how state courts had handled cases concerning right to counsel.

The year 1966 was an extraordinarily busy time for Dorsen. In addition to his teaching and administrative responsibilities at New York University, he was completing a casebook (with Thomas Emerson and David Haber) on civil and political liberties and acting as the reporter and draftsman for a model anti-discrimination statute that he was scheduled to defend in July before the Commissioners on Uniform State Laws. The statute was designed to continue at the state level the revolution in American law initiated by the 1964 Civil Rights Act. He had also recently married, was planning to move to a more respectable apartment with his wife, and would soon learn that he was going to become a father. Dorsen had to fit his pro bono work on *Gault* into an already tight professional and personal schedule.

Mainzer and Dorsen began working on the jurisdictional statement shortly after the Supreme Court heard oral arguments for the first time in a juvenile justice case, *Kent v. United States.* The case involved the decision by District of Columbia Juvenile Court Judge Ketcham to transfer sixteen-year-old Morris Kent, an African American youth, to the criminal justice system for prosecution. Kent was charged with several counts of housebreaking, robbery, and rape. The District of Columbia police described him as a "one-man crime wave." Judge Ketcham had studied the notoriously difficult issue of which juveniles should be transferred to criminal court. In 1959, he had issued a policy memorandum to the staff of the D.C. Juvenile Court that laid out the "determinative facts" judges should take into account before deciding that the Juvenile Court would "waive its jurisdiction" and transfer a juvenile offender to criminal court. Ketcham did not believe that Kent, who had many prior arrests and was charged with violent crimes, belonged in the juvenile justice system. The primary issue on appeal in *Kent* involved statutory interpretation, whether the D.C. Juvenile Court had applied correctly the relevant congressional law, but it potentially raised constitutional questions about the standards used in waiver proceedings. Did the juvenile court, for instance, have to follow the due process standards required in an administrative, civil, or criminal case? Did there have to be a hearing? Did the juvenile have a right to counsel?

Before Kent's criminal trial and during the appeals process, his court-appointed attorney, Mark Sandground, had his client evaluated for sixty days at the District of Columbia General Hospital. The hospital reported that Kent suffered from schizophrenia and may have been psychotic at the time of his crimes. The psychiatrists for the prosecution also found him mentally ill, but determined that he was capable of standing trial. Kent lost his appeal of the juvenile court's waiver decision and was tried in criminal court. During the trial, the prosecution conceded that Kent might not have been criminally responsible for the rapes. The argument was that he had intentionally sought to rob the women's apartments, but once he found a woman alone in bed at night he could not stop himself from raping her. A jury convicted Kent on the housebreaking and robbery charges, but acquitted him by reason of insanity of the rape charges. The judge sentenced him to serve thirty to ninety years in prison. Sandground appealed Kent's conviction to the D.C. Circuit Court of Appeals. The circuit court held that the juvenile court's decision to transfer Kent had correctly followed the statutory guidelines and thus the criminal court had had jurisdiction over his case.

After the Supreme Court agreed to hear oral arguments in *Kent*, Professor Nicholas Kittrie of American University filed an amicus brief on the behalf of thirteen individual sponsors. First among the sponsors—and not just alphabetically—was the Honorable Thurman Arnold, an iconic figure in American law and the only Washington lawyer to have a building named after him. After a brief stint as a federal circuit court judge, Arnold founded the prestigious law firm Arnold & Fortas. When Abe Fortas joined the Supreme Court in 1965, the firm became Arnold & Porter. Arnold and the other sponsors argued that *Kent* raised one central question: "to what extent traditional constitutional guarantees apply to juvenile court proceedings." This question mattered because the nation's juvenile courts heard more than a million cases a year. They added, "The present case not only provides an opportunity for the necessary definition of constitutional standards in juvenile court but indeed demands it." Even though the case rested on what lawyers call "bad facts"—fingerprints placed Kent at the crime scenes and his victims described him beating, raping, and threatening to kill them—these distinguished friends of the court implored the justices to use *Kent* to establish national standards for due process in juvenile court.

Representing the United States, Solicitor General Thurgood Marshall argued that *Kent* raised no constitutional questions but rather addressed only the proper interpretation of a congressional law for the District of Columbia. The United States' brief noted the growing concerns among experts about the administration of juvenile justice, citing first Judge Ketcham's chapter in Rosenheim's *Justice for the Child*. Yet the brief high-lighted that the District of Columbia already provided ample due process protection in juvenile court. "Indeed, many of the constitutional problems being debated in other jurisdictions are already settled in the District of Columbia. Thus, an accused juvenile in the District is entitled to a jury trial on the issue of delinquency." The brief reiterated the protections ju-veniles received in criminal courts: "It is also settled in this jurisdiction that no statement obtained from a juvenile prior to waiver of jurisdiction is admissible in a subsequent criminal trial . . . and that a juvenile has the right to counsel at delinquency hearings." Consequently, the respondents dismissed the constitutional question of the amicus brief, concluding, "The only Juvenile Court question presented here is a narrow one: Was the Juvenile Court's waiver of jurisdiction accomplished in compliance with the statute and without fundamental unfairness to petitioner?"

Among the justices deciding *Kent* was Abe Fortas. President Johnson had nominated Fortas, a longtime friend and advisor, to the bench in 1965. Johnson and Fortas were also close friends with Elizabeth Wickenden, and Fortas shared her interest in social welfare law. On March 21, 1966, the

Supreme Court announced its 5–4 decision in *Kent*. Writing for the majority, Fortas propitiously provided Dorsen and Mainzer with a framework for their jurisdictional statement in *Gault*.

In *Kent*, Fortas made two separate arguments about juvenile justice. First, he described "the special protections and provisions of the Juvenile Court Act" as an entitlement that could not be taken away without due process. If the juvenile court had retained its jurisdiction, then Kent could have received a maximum of five years of treatment before he turned twenty-one and aged out of the system. Once he was transferred to the criminal court, he faced the possibility of the death sentence. Thus, the waiver decision was "critically important" because it stripped Kent of his protected status as a minor. According to Fortas, "We do not consider whether, on the merits, Kent should have been transferred; but there is no place in our system of law for reaching a result of such tremendous consequences without ceremony—without hearing, without effective assistance of counsel, without a statement of reasons. It is inconceivable that a court of justice dealing with adults, with respect to a similar issue, would proceed in this manner." He added, "It would be extraordinary if society's special concern for children, as reflected in the District of Columbia's Juvenile Court Act, permitted this procedure. We hold that it does not."

This first argument is an example of what the law professor Franklin Zimring later described as the diversionary rationale for juvenile justice. According to this legal theory, the primary role of the juvenile court is to divert children and youth from the harsh punishment meted out by the criminal justice system. Adding due process protection to a waiver hearing, as the sponsors of the amicus brief contended, would strengthen the juvenile court because these protections reinforced the importance of having a less punitive system for juveniles.

Fortas then questioned whether the Progressive Era rationale for the procedural informality of juvenile justice could still be justified. This assumption, he noted, had been rooted in the philosophy of social welfare, not law. Moreover, it had led the United States Appellate Court for the District of Columbia to hold that a child could claim "only the fundamental due process right to fair treatment." Drawing on similar arguments, other appellate courts had held that juveniles were not entitled to bail, indictment by grand jury, speedy and public trial, trial by jury, immunity against self-incrimination, confrontation of accusers, and the right to counsel. But had this procedural informality benefitted minors? Had it contributed to children and their families' receiving the social services that they needed?

In his most famous statement in *Kent,* Fortas acknowledged that the modern juvenile justice system was fundamentally flawed. Fortas declared, "There is evidence, in fact, that there may be grounds for concern that the child receives the worst of both worlds: that he gets neither the protections accorded to adults nor the solicitous care and regenerative treatment postulated for children." Fortas nonetheless heeded the solicitor general's argument and declined "the invitation [by amicus curiae] to rule that constitutional guaranties which would be applicable to adults charged with the serious offenses for which Kent was tried must be applied in juvenile court proceedings with allegations of law violation." Instead, the Supreme Court remanded Kent's case to the district court to determine whether his transfer had been proper, noting "that if that Court finds the waiver inappropriate, petitioner's conviction must be vacated."

Significantly, the four dissenting justices—Hugo Black, John Marshall Harlan, Potter Stewart, and Byron White—made no effort to contest the substance of Fortas's opinion. Instead, they objected only to the majority's decision to remand the case to the District of Columbia. Writing for the four dissenters, Justice Stewart contended that the case should have instead been remanded to the Court of Appeals for the District of Columbia Circuit. Through silence, they neither confirmed nor denied Fortas's assertion that children might be experiencing "the worst of both worlds."

The Supreme Court, however, decided *Kent* on statutory grounds. This meant that the holding applied only to the District of Columbia. Still, Fortas's opinion read like a prologue to a constitutional drama. The ACLU lawyers believed that *Gault* should become Act One.

Two weeks after the Supreme Court announced its *Kent* decision, Mainzer and Dorsen had reworked the "Questions Presented" section of the jurisdictional statement to emphasize one question:

Whether the Juvenile Code of Arizona . . . on its face or as construed and applied, is invalid under the Due Process Clause of the Fourteenth Amendment to the United States Constitution because it authorizes a juvenile to be taken from the custody of his parents and to be committed to a state institution by a judicial proceeding which confers unlimited discretion upon the Juvenile Court and dispenses with the following procedural safeguards required by due process of law:

1. right to notice of the charges of delinquency;
2. right to counsel;
3. right to confrontation and cross-examination of adverse witnesses;
4. privilege against self-incrimination;
5. right to a transcript of the proceedings; and
6. right to appellate review of the juvenile court's decision.

In explaining why this question was substantial, they repeatedly referenced Justice Fortas's freshly minted opinion in *Kent* and made their case for Gault by quoting Fortas's damning statement, "There is evidence, that there may be grounds for concern that the child receives the worst of both worlds."

The same day Mainzer and Dorsen completed the "questions presented," Wulf mailed them the Mississippi Supreme Court decision in *Interest of Long* (1966), which held "that the right to counsel attaches in juvenile proceedings." He added, "Like most Mississippi Supreme Court opinions, it is something less than scholarly. But on the other hand, if Mississippi holds that juveniles are entitled to counsel, I would think that every other state in the Union would be ashamed to do otherwise."

On May 2, 1966, Melvin Wulf filed the Jurisdictional Statement with the Clerk of the Supreme Court and wired the $100 processing fee. The listing of appellant's attorneys reflected the changes that had brought Gault's case to the Supreme Court. Norman Dorsen took the lead position, followed by Wulf. Amelia Lewis, who had originally brought the case to the attention of the ACLU followed Wulf and was misidentified as "Amelie." Charles Ares and Gertrude Mainzer were listed as "of counsel." The ACLU then issued a press release announcing that it had "urged the United States Supreme Court to review an Arizona Supreme Court decision denying children the due process protections guaranteed by the Bill of Rights." The case, according to the news release, was straightforward: "Charging that the Arizona Juvenile Code violates the Fourteenth Amendment due process clause, the civil liberties group filed a jurisdictional statement with the high court on behalf of Paul and Marjorie Gault, whose 15-year-old son, Gerald, was committed as a delinquent to the Arizona Industrial School in June, 1964, for the offense of 'lewd phone calls.'" Now they had to wait and see whether the Supreme Court would agree to hear *Gault.*

Since other juvenile justice cases were working their way through the nation's court systems, it was likely that the Supreme Court would combine cases from several states and hear them together. The Supreme Court, however, decided to hear only *Gault.* On June 20, 1966, Melvin Wulf received the good news. The clerk laid out the procedural requirements: "This is to advise you, as provided by Rule 41, that the above-entitled case will not be reached for argument until next term, and accordingly the petitioner's (appellant's) brief will not be due until next August 25th, or thirty days after receipt of the printed record, whichever date is later." In a letter to Amelia Lewis, Wulf was elated. "We are getting to work right away on the *Gault* brief. It is going to be a great case."

Several issues had to be addressed almost immediately. Should the ACLU take the hard-line position that the Constitution required juvenile courts to be functionally equivalent to criminal courts and require all the same due process protections? Or should the ACLU focus primarily on securing the right to counsel as an opening wedge? In the wake of *Gideon,* this would be the easiest but narrowest path to victory. Once the ACLU lawyers determined their own strategy, they could work with the general counsels of other interested organizations that could file amicus briefs raising complementary issues. Ultimately, the American Parents Committee (a public service association that worked on federal legislation for children), the Legal Aid Society and Citizens' Committee for Children of New York, and the National Legal Aid and Defender Association (NLADA) filed briefs supporting the ACLU. The National Council of Juvenile Judges initially considered filing a brief to support the ACLU's position but chose not to participate in the case.

After a preliminary meeting, the ACLU lawyers (Wulf, Dorsen, Mainzer, and Ares, who visited New York) decided to emphasize a litany of basic constitutional guarantees but not to take the hard-line position. Appellate counsel for the NLADA Leon Polsky attended the meeting and reported that the ACLU would emphasize "right to counsel, right to notice of charges and right to confrontation of witnesses, and possibly self-incrimination." Yet he was "concerned that Gault's counsel are not going far enough, although in the context of their representation of the client these issues are the ones presented by the case for consideration." The facts of *Gault* limited the appellant's argument. A friend of the court brief could go further, however. Polsky contended that NLADA should take "the hard line position that the whole bundle of criminal process should attach to these proceedings and that where an act otherwise criminal is the basis for the juvenile court proceeding the standards of proofs should be the criminal one." He added, "Whether the Court will reach and decide the questions I have suggested as the basis for the *amicus* position is problematical; however I believe the position must be stated so that it not go by default."

Once the ACLU settled on its strategy, Melvin Wulf hired James Murray, an associate at Chabourne, Parke, Whiteside & Wolff, to complete an initial draft of the brief over the summer. Dorsen had to complete his casebook and defend his anti-discrimination statute in July before he could turn his full attention to the case. Wulf also called Alice Freer, a program analyst in the Office of the Director of Juvenile Delinquency Service, to request copies of the amicus curiae brief in *Kent* and other relevant materials. She provided the ACLU with copies of all the studies of juvenile courts sponsored by the federal government.

Meanwhile, Dorsen wrote to Solicitor General Thurgood Marshall and his friend and attorney general of the United States, Nicholas Katzenbach, to ask the United States to file an amicus brief supporting the ACLU's position. He sent copies of these letters to Melvin Wulf and observed, "I suppose there is no harm in trying." He added, "I take this opportunity to raise the question of oral argument. As I suggested at the luncheon, I really would like to argue this case myself. In view of my position, as well as the years of work I have put in for the Union without the chance to argue, it seems to me that this is not unreasonable." Wulf agreed. Norman Dorsen would have his opportunity to argue a case before the Supreme Court.

The United States, however, declined Dorsen's invitation to file an amicus brief supporting the appellant. Attorney General Katzenbach, a former student of Abe Fortas's at Yale Law School, was concerned that the due process revolution threatened to undermine effective law enforcement. In a 1965 address to the Annual Meeting of the Law Alumni Association of the University of Chicago, Katzenbach cautioned, for example, against placing too many restraints on police officers. He acknowledged that the recent reports of the Committee on Poverty and the Administration of Criminal Justice (known as the Allen Committee for its chairman, law professor Francis Allen) had revealed how much the law in practice differed from the law on the books. Yet he believed law professors had learned the wrong lesson from this finding. Instead of using theory to change practice, they should study how practice could help refine theory. To drive home his point, he told a story about Norman Dorsen.

> Let me illustrate by a story—one that is quite true and not apocryphal. It concerns a young law professor from New York, active in the civil liberties field, who drove up to Harvard to visit a colleague. He left his briefcase in his car and on returning was shocked to find it gone.
>
> Terribly agitated, he called the police. Two patrolmen arrived, soothed him, and assured him that they would find the briefcase before it was thrown in some dustbin. They strolled up the shady street, past a decrepit car and nearby discovered a man peering into other cars.
>
> The police stopped the man, frisked him, and ordered him to return with them to the old car, which he admitted was his. They made him open the trunk. Inside was the briefcase.
>
> The agitated young professor grabbed the man and shook him, shouting "Why did you do this?" "Don't you realize there are months of irreplaceable work in that briefcase?"
>
> The professor's concern was understandable. In his briefcase was the only copy of a long paper he had written on New York's stop-and-frisk law—attacking the law.

Katzenbach explained the point of the story: "There might well be areas of law that cannot be formalized without excess rigidity. We could not, for instance, provide legal rules for business enterprise, or police detection, or the life of the Senate. There are some aspects of justice that may have to be left to intuition, imagination and a complex interplay of personality." Whether the attorney general or solicitor general believed that juvenile courts were such an aspect of the law is unclear, but the United States chose not to participate on either side in *Gault*.

Before turning his undivided attention to *Gault*, Dorsen completed his work on *Political and Civil Liberties in the United States* on July 20, 1966, and then travelled the following week to Montreal to defend his draft of an Anti-Discrimination Act before the National Conference of Commissioners on Uniform State Laws. By a 23-to-17 vote, the commissioners agreed to promulgate it as a "Model Act." In a letter to Ares, Dorsen shared his observations about William Rehnquist, an Arizona lawyer who had clerked for Supreme Court Justice Robert Jackson in the early 1950s.

Then in private practice but active in Arizona politics, Rehnquist would later become an associate justice (1972 to 1986) and then chief justice of the Supreme Court (1986 to 2005). Dorsen wrote, "You will not be surprised to learn that Rehnquist, who as you may know is an Arizona Commissioner, was very much in evidence on the floor with cutting-down suggestions. No major damage done, and one or two of his ideas were acceptable. He struck me as fairly smart, or at least shrewd, conservative, and basically not a nice guy. Good luck with him!"

After a productive summer, on August 30, 1966, Dorsen received a complete copy of James Murray's twenty-four page draft of the *Gault* brief and all the supporting materials. The draft was rudimentary and rough. Its introduction contained only three sentences. "The Fourteenth Amendment forbids 'any State' to 'deprive any person of . . . liberty . . . without due process of law. The protection is not just of citizens or adults, but of 'any person.' The standard of 'due process of law' is required whenever the effect of the State action is to deprive one of 'liberty' through whatever mode, whether denominated criminal, civil or exercise of *parens patriae*."

The first section, "Facts of Deprivation in this Case," was dry and inaccurate. It misstated the maximum sentence under Arizona law for an adult convicted of using lewd language and asserted that Gerald was still incarcerated. Dorsen later repeated this mistaken assumption that Gerald was still confined in the Arizona Industrial School for Boys during his oral argument before the Supreme Court, when, in fact, Gerald had been released in November 1965 to live with his parents, though the school retained its jurisdiction over him.

The subsequent sections, "The History of Deprivation in Juvenile Court Proceedings" and "The Recognition of Due Process Standards in Juvenile Court Proceedings," were the most developed parts of the brief but lacked polish. For example, the historical section began, "The widespread existence of anomalous proceedings as this in otherwise civilized country demands an examination of the background and development of the juvenile courts." The final section "Specific Rights of General Application Denied in this Case" briefly explained the absence of notice, counsel, confrontation, and appeal, but Murray had left the section on self-incrimination blank. It would be up to Dorsen to turn this preliminary draft into a first-rate brief. He had three weeks. He recruited Daniel Rezneck, a former law clerk to William Brennan and an associate at Arnold & Porter, to help him.

Dorsen had never met Gerald Gault or his parents. In those days, appellate attorneys rarely met their clients. Dorsen instead used the record from the habeas corpus hearing to craft a compelling constitutional story about the Gaults' experience with an arbitrary and unjust legal system. That story became the "Statement of the Case." It began with Gerald's arrest on June 8, 1964, and concluded with Judge McGhee's inability during the August habeas corpus hearing to explain precisely why he had found the boy delinquent. This five-page narrative prepared the reader for a four-page summary of the argument, followed by fifty pages of legal analysis that cited leading authorities on juvenile justice and the relevant case law.

Dorsen's legal argument unfolded in two parts. First, he argued that the benevolent ideal of *parens patriae* that led to the "bartering of due process for individualized treatment has cost juveniles dearly." They now experienced the "worst of both worlds" described by Fortas in *Kent*. Arizona's law and practice followed this older ideal. Thus, "this brief will try to demonstrate that the petitioner in this case, like countless other juveniles in Arizona and other jurisdictions, has in fact been receiving the 'worst of both worlds' in plain derogation of the requirements of the due process clause of the Fourteenth Amendment."

Second, he pointed out that modern juvenile court laws, such as the Standard Juvenile Court Act (1959), the California Juvenile Court Law (1961), and the New York Family Court (1962) all substituted "fundamental fairness" for discredited notions of state paternalism. They did so, Dorsen explained, due to "compelling reasons of fairness and authority to provide young people with fundamental protections in juvenile court." Children, just like adults, needed to be protected from arbitrary injustice. Otherwise, innocent children would be found guilty and improperly punished.

Dorsen also subtly connected Jerry Gault's case to the civil rights movement and the question of political liberties. In a lengthy footnote, Dorsen pointed out, "Absence of procedural safeguards affects not only the reliability of juvenile proceedings but permits arbitrary disposition of young people who will not 'cooperate' or who are involved in unpopular social movements." He added, "Juveniles, for example, have comprised a large proportion of those who in the past decade have peacefully demonstrated for their civil rights and have been unlawfully arrested for asserting constitutionally protected rights. The treatment accorded to these minor Negroes in juvenile courts demonstrates the capacity of juvenile courts to punish for reasons unrelated to their individual welfare." He directed the justices to the U.S. Commission on Civil Rights Report on Law Enforcement that concluded, "local authorities used the broad definition afforded them by the absence of safeguards [in juvenile proceedings] to impose excessively harsh treatment on juveniles." For a Supreme Court sympathetic to the civil rights movement, it made sense to draw this connection between civil and political liberties.

Recognizing the harm that the persistence of the notion that lawyers were detrimental to juvenile court proceedings could do to his due process argument, Dorsen worked to allay those fears. He incorporated extensive testimony from Charles Schinitsky, who had founded the Juvenile Rights Division of the New York Legal Aid Society in 1961. Schinitsky demonstrated that lawyers representing minors in juvenile court in New York City had not had an adverse impact on the system and actually helped the judges to run their courts more smoothly. Dorsen also cited government studies to support this assertion.

Dorsen then proceeded to use Gerald's specific case to show what could happen to any child in America who was denied the basic due process protections of notice; right to counsel, confrontation and cross-examination; privilege against self-incrimination; appellate review; and a right to a transcript. Because 36 percent of the American population in 1965 was subject to the jurisdiction of juvenile courts, potentially millions of children and their families could experience similar constitutional deprivations. In conclusion, Dorsen stated, "The judgment of the Supreme Court of Arizona should be reversed with instructions to grant a writ of habeas corpus ordering the release from custody of Gerald Francis Gault."

The state of Arizona had to respond to Dorsen and defend the decision of its supreme court. The Office of the Attorney General of Arizona was responsible for preparing the state's defense. Attorney General Darrell Smith delegated this responsibility to Assistant Attorney General Frank Parks. Parks was thirty-one years old, had graduated from George Washington University Law School, and had been practicing law for a year and a half. Like Dorsen, Parks would have an opportunity to make an oral argument before the Warren Court. Unlike Dorsen, who had worked at the Supreme Court and knew the justices well, Parks was an outsider. Dorsen also had the advantage of *Kent,* which he could use to argue that the theory of *parens patriae* had already been discredited. By contrast, Parks had to defend this traditional approach because it served as a legal foundation for the Arizona Juvenile Code and the Arizona Supreme Court's decision in *Gault.*

Although *Kent* placed Parks at a disadvantage, he could contest the ACLU's constitutional story that Gerald Gault was a boy who received a prison sentence for only making a lewd phone call. Accordingly, Parks used his "Statement of the Case" to tell a very different story, one beginning in July 1962, when Gerald had been first accused of theft. Parks then emphasized that two years later, Gerald was again arrested, this time for grand theft. He explained that Judge McGhee had placed Gerald on probation and warned his family of the consequences of violating this court order. Gerald was still on probation, Parks pointed out, when he was apprehended for making a lewd phone call on June 8, 1964. Gerald had thus committed an offense while on probation. Parks argued that this pattern of delinquency, not a first offense, had landed him in the Arizona State Industrial School.

Though Parks did an admirable job of explaining that the Arizona juvenile justice system incorporated elements of due process, he ultimately would need five justices of the U.S. Supreme Court to agree that *parens patriae* "remains a sound and purposeful doctrine." The constitutional law experts he consulted told him that post-*Kent,* this was going to be a hard sell. Helping Parks in this effort was the Ohio Association of Juvenile Judges, which filed the only amicus brief supporting the state of Arizona.

The Ohio brief did not help much. It reiterated the Progressive Era argument about the benevolence of the juvenile court as a social welfare institution and argued that Arizona juvenile justice was not punitive. As the brief stated, "The Arizona Industrial School, to which this lad was committed (not sentenced), is not a 'penal' institution, but rather a 'school'—a place of learning—which the state, as *parens patriae,* furnishes for youth found to be in need of the specialized care and treatment available there, in the same manner as any wise parent would provide hospitalization for a sick child." The authors of the brief also included mean-spirited language about Mrs. Gault. They wrote, "Mrs. Gault's original affidavit states that she thought she needed an attorney, but rather than consulting one, she discussed the matter with the Chief of Police. This is an example of one of the professional advantages the physicians have over the attorneys. If a cancer victim consults the corner druggist instead of a doctor for advice, they just bury him."

Also, inexplicably, in a brief devoted to touting the virtues of *parens patriae*, the authors used legal standards from criminal law to find Gerald Gault guilty. They stated, "Admittedly, Gerald placed the call, and thus, both practically and under the most rigid requirements of the criminal law, was *particeps criminis*, and fully chargeable with all that was said, regardless of who said it. Gerald's admissions were tantamount to a guilty plea in the criminal court and hence there was no need for witnesses or sworn testimony." Arguments that blended juvenile and criminal law were not going to help Parks convince the Supreme Court to reject its characterization of the modern juvenile court in *Kent*.

The Ohio brief did make one potentially helpful argument. Lewd phone calls were a serious matter. The authors cited a campaign by AT&T (then the only phone company in the United States) against obscene calls and an article, "Terror by Telephone." The article reported that more than 46,000 complaints about prank phone calls had been filed in a single month and that hundreds of thousands of these calls went unreported. Although the brief failed to develop this point, the question of whether Gerald had made "sex" calls before would later be raised by Chief Justice Earl Warren during the oral argument in *Gault*.

Frank Parks would have been better served if Roger Baldwin had filed an amicus brief. Baldwin, who had opposed the ACLU's use of *Gault* to attack the juvenile court, objected to the brief for the appellants. In a memo to Dorsen and Wulf, he accused them of ignoring "the practical work of the courts in protesting its abuses" but acknowledged, "Of course judges with such wide powers often are high-handed or ignorant in treatment of delinquency." Yet he contended, "Only a very small proportion of children who come before the courts are taken from parents or committed to institutions. To set up due process procedures, with lawyers, records, examinations of witnesses etc. for all cases would transform the whole spirit of the courts." Instead, he proposed the following: Reserve such protections "only for cases in which a judge contemplates separation from parents. Then on his own motion or on the parents' request, a hearing de novo [from the beginning] with all due process could be held. Perhaps more fairly before another judge, surely if requested by the parents." Baldwin preferred a middle ground between absolute *parens patriae* and complete criminal due process.

Baldwin was not the only member of the ACLU angered by the association's brief. Amelia Lewis wrote to Norman Dorsen and Melvin Wulf to express her frustration at being left out of the process. In a letter acknowledging receipt of six copies of the brief, she explained, "I should have felt of better stature in the case had I received a copy of the proof sent to the printer so that I might have examined the same at that time. I would not have had reason to make any suggestions, I think, but I would have felt I was doing something along with you on this great job." In a postscript, she added, "The misspelling of the final a on my first name is a typo that should not be noted." It was a visual reminder that Amelia Lewis was no longer in the loop.

Both Dorsen and Wulf apologized to Lewis. Dorsen explained, "The only excuse we have—but at the time it seemed a compelling one—was that we fell behind schedule in the preparation of the brief, and we even had to have a week's extension. In short, it was a madhouse here, and we did not see a proof until three days before the brief was filed in the Court." He added, "Nevertheless, we should have been more alert about your participation. Needless to say, none of this would have been possible without you, and no matter who did the brief, it is you who deserve primary credit for bringing this case to the Supreme Court and to the eye of the public and profession." In partial recompense, the ACLU paid Lewis's expenses to fly to Washington, D.C., to watch the oral arguments in *Gault* that December.

After reading Arizona's brief in October, Dorsen realized that he did not know enough about juvenile reformatories. In a letter to Ares, Dorsen explained, "Traute suggested, and I agree, that we could use in a reply brief a written statement of the conditions at the type of 'Industrial School' in which Gault and others are confined. The idea, of course, is to show that the confinement is not a pleasant sojourn, but has elements of criminal punishment." It took Mainzer, a survivor of Bergen-Belsen, to suggest that the *Gault* litigation needed to include discussion of the conditions of imprisonment. Mainzer, who later became a family court judge in New York City, never forgot a lesson she learned during the Holocaust. "Everybody thinks freedom is something inborn, but it isn't. It is something that has to be taught and experienced."

By hiring Mainzer as a research associate for the Project on Social Welfare Law and listening to her advice, Dorsen demonstrated his wise judgment. Their efforts to develop this new frontier of civil liberties also explains why, during the final rush to complete the *Gault* brief, Dorsen took the time to write Abe Fortas. The brief letter was a testament to legal liberalism at its zenith.

Dear Mr. Justice Fortas:

Elizabeth Wickenden recently sent me a copy of your talk this summer before the Second Circuit Judicial Conference. As far as I know, you are the first member of the Court to address himself squarely to the problem of welfare law, and the social revolution that is providing the underpinning for legal change.

We are planning to include your remarks in a forthcoming issue of the Welfare Law Bulletin, which as you may know we have been publishing since last December.

Speaking from the perspective of an urban law school, it is truly remarkable how much student and professional interest has been generated by "Wicky's Revolution." As many students are getting involved in work connected with welfare law as any other subject at our Law School.

Dorsen had no need to mention that he would soon stand before Mr. Justice Fortas and his brethren to argue *In re Gault.* They knew he was coming.

CHAPTER 4

"It Will Be Known as the Magna Carta for Juveniles"

The U.S. Supreme Court announced its decision to review *In re Gault* near the end of its due process revolution (1961–1968). The court was nationalizing criminal procedure by extending protections in the Bill of Rights to the accused and defendants in state criminal courts, which heard more than 99 percent of the criminal cases in the United States. In his book *The Self-Inflicted Wound* (1970), the Supreme Court correspondent for *The New York Times* Fred Graham took stock of this unfolding revolution. As Graham noted, "History has played cruel jokes before, but few can compare with the coincidence in timing between the rise in crime, violence and racial tensions in the United States and the Supreme Court's campaign to strengthen the rights of criminal suspects against the state." He added, "[The Supreme] Court had announced the most rigid legal limitations that any society had sought to impose on its police at a time when the United States had the most serious crime problem of any so-called advanced nation in the world." According to the FBI's crime index, during the 1960s reported murders had increased by 52 percent, rapes by 84 percent, robbery by 144 percent, and aggravated assault by 86 percent.

Many Americans accused the Supreme Court of legislating from the bench, handcuffing the police, and coddling criminals. Alabama Governor George Wallace, a defiant segregationist who would run for president several times, popularized this critique. Wallace blamed the Great Society and legal liberalism for the nation's racial unrest and crime wave and vilified the Warren Court. He asserted, "The same Supreme Court that ordered integration and encouraged civil right legislation" was now "bending over backwards to help criminals." He added, "If a criminal knocks you over the head on your way home from work, he will be out of jail before you're out of the hospital and the policeman who arrested him will be on trial. . . . Some psychologist will say, well, he's not to blame, society is to blame." Other politicians, such as Arizona Senator Barry Goldwater and, later, Richard Nixon, learned how to frame crime as a national issue.

In his acceptance speech at the Republican National Convention in 1964, Goldwater stated that "law and order" was a central theme of his presidential campaign. He declared,

> Tonight there is violence in our streets, corruption in our highest offices, aimlessness among our youth, anxiety among our elderly. . . . Security from domestic violence, no less than from foreign aggression, is the most elementary form and fundamental purpose of any government, and a government that cannot fulfill this purpose is one that cannot command the loyalty of its citizens. History shows us that nothing prepares the way for tyranny more than the failure of public officials to keep the streets safe from bullies and marauders. We Republicans seek a government that attends to . . . enforcing law and order.

As the criminologist Jonathan Simon has noted, "Democrat Lyndon Johnson beat Goldwater handily but wasted no time in declaring 'war on crime' as part of his Great Society." In July 1965, Johnson established the President's Commission on Law Enforcement and Administration of Justice. He appointed Attorney General Nicholas Katzenbach to chair it. The commission included a special task force devoted to studying juvenile delinquency and youth crime. The Supreme Court, as it turned out, would incorporate the task force's findings into its *Gault* decision. Before that could occur, however, the Supreme Court announced a decision that enraged Wallace, Goldwater, and others who believed that criminals were gaining unfair advantages.

On June 13, 1966, Chief Justice Earl Warren announced the Supreme Court's 5–4 decision in *Miranda v. Arizona,* which held that police officers must advise defendants of their constitutional rights before interrogating them. Abe Fortas, the newest member of the court, had cast the fifth and decisive vote. He joined the chief justice, Hugo Black, William O. Douglas, and William Brennan. As Graham explained, "This decision said that no statement made by a person being held by the police could be used in court unless the suspect had first been offered and had turned down the assistance of a lawyer—who, the Court conceded, would undoubtedly tell the suspect not to say anything." *Miranda* ignited a firestorm. Graham reported, "The Supreme Court's trumpet call for justice had been heard as a call for permissiveness in dealing with criminals, and *Miranda v. Arizona* became the cutting edge of a political thrust against the Warren Court." Exactly one week after delivering its *Miranda* decision, the Supreme Court announced that it would hear *Gault*.

Because the Supreme Court was asked to review *Gault* on direct appeal, the justices were compelled to hear the case if it presented a substantial federal question. The court had complete discretion whether to hear cases arising from certiorari petitions and denied most of these appeals. In a memo, Fortas's law clerk John Griffiths explained that if *Gault* were a certiorari petition, then "I would deny on the ground this is too murky a case to take as the first one in which to extend Kent to the states. However, as an appeal, it seems to me absolutely impossible to deny that substantial federal questions are presented as to the applicability of the due process clause, and more specific constitutional requirements, to the states." Fortas and his brethren agreed and accepted the case, and the clerk scheduled oral arguments for early December.

Norman Dorsen worked closely with Daniel Rezneck to prepare. They decided to use the facts in *Gault* to their advantage. They scripted a concise opening statement that introduced the procedural due process issues (right to counsel, adequate notice, confrontation and cross-examination; privilege against self-incrimination; and the right to a transcript and appellate review) and recapped how the case had made its way through the Arizona court system. For their final sentence, they wanted the justices to know what the absence of due process meant for their client: "Gerald is still in confinement and has been for two and one half years." They did not know that this statement was false. The legal record had not revealed that Gerald had been on home placement for more than a year.

After the brief introduction, Dorsen would then slowly walk the justices through the legal process that ultimately led to Gerald's incarceration. This narrative would set the stage for him to make the case for requiring juvenile courts to follow specific due process requirements. He would begin, "The facts are relatively simple and yet it is not possible to be confident about exactly what happened at the original proceeding." This casual remark so early in his argument prepared the justices to recognize that the absence of a recorded transcript was a fundamental failing arising from the informality of the Arizona juvenile court process. Because there were no transcripts of the juvenile court hearings, Dorsen would explain that he had to rely instead on the transcript of the habeas corpus hearing to piece together what had happened in the Gila County Juvenile Court.

On the morning of December 6, 1966, in the lawyer's room in the Supreme Court building, Dorsen and Reznek held their final strategy session. They were confident that Dorsen would win the votes of at least five justices but wanted all nine. To secure them, Dorsen had to carefully navigate the treacherous waters of the incorporation debate. This debate involved an unsettled legal historical question about the adoption of the Fourteenth Amendment to the U.S. Constitution in 1868. Justices disagreed about whether the amendment had incorporated the protections of personal rights and liberties from the Bill of Rights into the new amendment's due process clause. If so, then the Fourteenth Amendment's command, "No State shall make or enforce any law which shall abridge the privileges or immunities of citizens of the United States . . . without due process of law" required state courts to follow the Bill of Rights. With several notable exceptions in First Amendment and parental rights cases, until 1961 the Supreme Court held that provisions from the Bill of Rights had not been incorporated into the Fourteenth Amendment.

The differences on the Court in how the Fourteenth Amendment should be interpreted emerged clearly in 1947, with *Adamson v. California*. While the majority in this case held that the privilege against self-incrimination did not apply to the states, Justice Hugo Black used his dissent to argue that it did. He advocated for the Supreme Court to adopt a theory of full incorporation that held every protection in the Bill of Rights applied to the states via the Fourteenth Amendment. He declared, "I would follow what I believe was the original purpose of the Fourteenth Amendment—to extend to all the people of the nation the complete protection of the Bill of Rights."

Justice Felix Frankfurter rejected both Black's historical interpretation of the original purpose of the Fourteenth Amendment and his theory of full incorporation. Instead, Frankfurter argued that the court should continue to use the fundamental fairness standard. This standard held that the due process clause of the Fourteenth Amendment required states only to abide by those procedural safeguards required for the fair administration of justice. Accordingly, Frankfurter contended that the Fourteenth

Amendment "neither comprehends the specific provisions by which the founders deemed it appropriate to restrict the federal government nor is it confined to them. The Due Process Clause of the Fourteenth Amendment has an independent potency." He explained that "the judicial process at its best—comprehensive briefs and powerful arguments on both sides, followed by long deliberation" was the proper method for the high court to determine the meaning of the due process clause.

After Frankfurter retired from the Supreme Court in 1962, Justice John Marshall Harlan became the standard bearer for fundamental fairness. At the same time, Justice William Brennan developed the theory known as "selective incorporation." Brennan's approach focused on whether a specific provision in the Bill of Rights, such as the privilege against self-incrimination, was a critical element necessary for a fair trial. If so, then the Court should read that provision into the Fourteenth Amendment. In 1963, Columbia University Law Professor Louis Henkin cautioned that selective incorporation was actually a strategic means to achieve the ends of total incorporation. By 1966, the Supreme Court had selectively incorporated much of the Bill of Rights into the Fourteenth Amendment.

Dorsen's goal was to avoid being dragged into the whirlpool of the incorporation debate. To do so, he worked to demonstrate that under any constitutional theory—whether total, fundamental fairness, or selective incorporation—juveniles required specific due process protections. Constitutionally, he argued, juveniles were entitled to counsel, notice, a right to confrontation and cross-examination, the privilege against self-incrimination, a transcript, and the right to appellate review of a juvenile court judge's decision.

As the counsel for the appellant, Dorsen would address the court first. Just before the case was called, Chief Judge of the U.S. Court of Appeals for the District of Columbia Circuit David Bazelon entered the crowded room. Bazelon was the most outspoken proponent of the due process revolution on the federal bench and a close friend of Brennan. Because all the seats were taken, he took a chair from the press gallery and carried it to the counsel's table. Bazelon, the embodiment of 1960s legal liberalism, sat down next to Dorsen.

Dorsen stepped to the podium and began his presentation. Remarkably, only two justices interrupted Dorsen during the first eleven minutes of his oral argument. Five minutes in, Potter Stewart asked whether Gerald had received notice of the charges against him. Stewart's question pinpointed an underlying tension in the case. Was Dorsen's theory that Arizona had violated the constitutional rights of Gerald Gault? Or was he instead arguing that the state had violated Paul and Marjorie Gault's parental rights? Dorsen avoided explaining his theory of the case at this stage by answering that neither Gerald nor his mother had received written notice of the charges. He then continued with his scripted narrative. Five minutes later, Justice Fortas asked the second question. He wanted to know what the maximum penalty under Arizona law was for an adult convicted of making lewd phone calls and how this compared with Gerald's punishment. Dorsen explained that Gerald could potentially be incarcerated for six years, whereas an adult could have been sentenced to only sixty days in jail and fined. He had confirmed Fortas's damning critique of modern juvenile justice in *Kent*.

Fortas's question prompted several justices, including Harlan, to inquire about the Arizona Industrial School for Boys. Harlan asked, "What is this industrial school, is it a prison?" Dorsen responded to his former boss, "Well of course I have not been there. It is a school where delinquent children are sent." He further explained that it was a secure facility. Chief Justice Earl Warren then stated, "The boy can't go home." Dorsen immediately agreed: "He can't go home. That is pretty clear. He can't go home until his minority ends unless the Board of Governors of the State Industrial School let him go home." Perhaps this part of the oral argument would have turned out differently if Dorsen and Warren had known that Gerald had already been released. In any case, Warren proceeded to ask one more question, "Has he ever done anything like this, making these telephone calls?" Dorsen replied that Gerald was on probation for being in the company of a boy who had stolen a wallet but had not made other obscene phone calls. Dorsen later recalled the confidence he felt after that exchange. Warren, he remembered, "leaned back, and the case was over, at least for him. If I had the nerve—I once did this in a lower court—I would have said, 'If there are no more questions,' and sat down."

Wisely, Dorsen proceeded to analyze how the Arizona Supreme Court in its "extensive opinion" had addressed each of the separate due process issues. Because the Arizona court had ruled on these specific issues, he argued that it was proper for the U.S. Supreme Court to review all of them. He then provided the justices with a brief historical overview of the Progressive Era juvenile court movement; it explained why these courts were established, their supporters' call for individualized justice for the child, and the theory of *parens patriae* that likened the state to a benevolent parent. This theory, he explained, had led jurists to reason that children were not entitled to basic due process protections in juvenile court. Now, he stressed, scholars and jurists had begun to question this assumption and were calling for more due process in juvenile court. "The climax," he pointed out, "came last year in *Kent v. United States*. Summing up the present situation, the Court said as follows: 'While there can be no doubt of the original laudable purpose of juvenile courts, studies and critiques in recent years raise serious questions as to whether actual performance measures well enough against theoretical purpose to make tolerable the immunity of the process from the reach of constitutional guaranties applicable to adults.'" He then quoted Fortas's condemnation of a system where children received the worst of both worlds.

Justice William O. Douglas interrupted Dorsen to point out that the Supreme Court had decided *Kent* on statutory grounds. The decision applied only to juvenile courts in the nation's capital. It looked like Dorsen would finally have to explain why the Supreme Court should extend its due process revolution to state juvenile courts. He explained that the court in *Kent* had reserved the constitutional question of due process in juvenile court and that it was now time to answer that question. "This case," Dorsen stated, "presents that issue in the five specific respects that I outlined above." Justices Fortas and Brennan, however, asked Dorsen first to address the theoretical basis for treating children in juvenile court differently from adults in criminal court. When Dorsen replied that there was no satisfactory explanation, Brennan asked about the legal argument that "the basic right of the juvenile is not to liberty, but custody." Dorsen replied, "We reject that." Brennan responded, "I know that you reject that, but does not that sum up the legal concept on which some of these rights are denied?" Dorsen conceded, "It may if I knew exactly what it meant." As Brennan continued to push him on this point, Dorsen re-emphasized that the concept's meaning had eluded him. "No matter how many times one says *parens patriae*," it still made no sense. Dorsen's responses meant that it would be up to Frank Parks to convince five justices that this concept had a place in American constitutional law.

Dorsen used the remainder of his time to remind the justices that his side was making a clear distinction between the determination of delinquency and the subsequent treatment of the child. They were not making any constitutional claims about what happened to a child after he was found delinquent. Instead, *Gault* was only about the adjudicatory stage. In Dorsen's analysis, one could preserve the juvenile court's mission of individual justice and therapeutic aims, while simultaneously safeguarding the constitutional rights of the child to due process. This approach promised the best of both worlds, procedural due process during the adjudicatory stage and the finest treatment and custodial care afterwards. To drive home this point, he singled out Justice Haydn Proctor's opinion in a New Jersey Supreme Court case decided only two weeks earlier. Proctor, a former acting governor of New Jersey and president of the state senate, argued that juveniles were entitled to a fair fact-finding process before being declared delinquent. Moreover, Dorsen explained that model juvenile court acts like New York's now established two separate hearings: an adjudicatory hearing and, if necessary, a dispositional hearing.

Dorsen then fielded questions from several justices. Those about the specifics of the New York Juvenile Code and other jurisdictions, Dorsen answered easily. The justices also asked him questions about due process protections that *Gault* had not raised, such as a right to a public trial. Dorsen emphasized that *Gault* did not raise these issues and suggested that there could be differences between juvenile and criminal courts to protect children. During this part of the oral argument, the justices questioned Dorsen as a colleague, and he answered in kind. "I am not sure," he said, "how I would decide that case." Justices Black and Harlan did try to get him to commit to the theory of total incorporation or fundamental fairness, but Dorsen avoided sailing too close to either the Scylla or Charybdis of the incorporation debate. Instead, he emphasized the facts and issues presented by *Gault*. He referred the justices to his brief, for example, and never explained during oral argument his theory about why juveniles were entitled to the privilege against self-incrimination.

Justice Tom Clark, who had voted with the majority in *Kent* but dissented in due process cases such as *Miranda*, raised the question of what would happen to the juvenile court if it became more like a criminal court. "Mr. Dorsen, if we accept your contention, what is left of the juvenile justice system?" Dorsen replied, "Mr. Justice Clark, the best part. The best part, of course, is rehabilitation and treatment, and all the rest." This answer was designed to allay the concerns of those who believed in traditional juvenile justice.

Dorsen closed by reminding the justices of the facts of *Gault* and the constitutional protections that Gerald had been denied. He highlighted that it was unclear, even in Judge McGhee's mind, why Gerald Gault had been found delinquent. He then answered the question that Justice Stewart had asked initially. "Even though Mrs. Gault knew of her right to retain counsel, that is far from protecting the right of counsel that we believe the Constitution requires. First of all, it is Gerald Gault's right, returning to a point that Mr. Justice Stewart alluded to this morning. Secondly, the right, we believe that is required by the Constitution, is the right is to assign counsel if the boy cannot afford it." He ended several minutes early, reserving time for a possible rebuttal to Frank Parks's oral argument. Parks, who had been told by constitutional experts that he would lose, was nervous. As he later recalled, "The question was, 'Just how badly would I lose?'"

Parks planned to use only fifty minutes of his allotted hour and reserved ten minutes for Merritt Green of the Ohio Association of Juvenile Court Judges to urge the high court to affirm the Arizona Supreme Court decision. Parks opened with the premise that juvenile court jurisprudence was at a crossroads. Two minutes later, Justice Byron White challenged this premise. The colloquy between Parks and White revealed that Parks was using Arizona to make broad generalizations about juvenile justice nationally.

> *White:* You think that this is such a big crossroads in this case for New York?
>
> *Parks:* [pause] Well, in my estimation of the New York provisions, your Honor, I believe that New York has gone beyond their crossroads.
>
> *White:* So this case is no crossroads for them? How about California?
>
> *Parks:* California, they have made an inroad on their crossroad, I believe while [interrupted by laughter] while I believe they haven't gone as far as the potential constitutional ramifications could conceivably take them.
>
> *White:* How about Illinois?
>
> *Parks:* [long pause] You're catching me short, Mr. Justice . . .
>
> *White:* You say this is a crossroads for the juvenile court system. Well that may be true in your state; this may be only true in certain states.
>
> *Parks:* In certain states. And, of course, I look through the monocle as seen through the state of Arizona, as to what our conception is of a proper and a proper functioning juvenile system.

The majority of justices on the Warren Court, however, did not want to view the case from Arizona's perspective.

Justice Fortas then forced Parks to explain why the specific due process rights that Dorsen said were constitutionally required would compromise the administration of juvenile justice in Arizona. He asked, "Let's see if that can be broken down a little bit. Will it interfere with individualized treatment, in the Arizona conception, for the child and the parent to be given written notice?" Parks replied, "Certainly not, certainly not." Fortas then asked: "Will it interfere with individualized treatment for counsel to be provided to them?" Parks tried to stop the line of questioning, "If you would wish, I will go into it now. I had hoped I might just provide the basic foundation for our reasoning." Fortas, however, persisted to ask about each of the due process provisions outlined by Dorsen.

Significantly, when the justices questioned Parks about the Arizona Industrial School, he corrected Dorsen's assertion that Gerald Gault was still incarcerated. He explained, "This leads me to a point that has not been brought out and I think will detract a bit from the harshness of the disposition that was made by the juvenile judge. Gerald Gault is no longer in the Fort Grant State Industrial School. Although he is still under their exclusive control and jurisdiction until he reaches his majority or he is absolutely released."

Though Parks was able to clarify the record on this one point, he had a difficult time with the constitutional questions. For example, Warren asked him why Arizona law allowed parents to retain counsel in juvenile court cases but did not provide counsel for those who could not afford to hire their own lawyer. Central to the Warren Court's Due Process Revolution was the ideal that the poor and wealthy should receive equal justice under the law. Accordingly, Warren questioned how Parks would distinguish

the situation where if a child of a wealthy family wants to bring a lawyer there to represent the child, they can do so and he can have representation all the way through the proceedings on the theory that it would be helpful to him, but on the other hand a poor family that cannot afford an attorney must remain bereft of one and must rely on the probation officer.

Post-*Gideon*, there was no acceptable constitutional answer to this question. Before he completed his portion of the oral argument, Parks was able to raise the significant point that there were no prosecutors in juvenile court. If states had to provide defense counsel for juveniles, they would presumably send prosecutors to juvenile court. This would most likely transform the juvenile court into an adversarial environment.

Merritt Green used his ten minutes to argue that the Supreme Court should not make the juvenile court into an imitation of adult criminal court. He observed, "This may be an oversimplification of a statement, but delinquency is not a crime. Children do not commit crimes. They become delinquent. They are not treated as crimes until the [juvenile] court that has the exclusive jurisdiction releases them to the adult court to be as an adult would be tried, as in the *Kent* case." He added, "The Court will remember that in the *Kent* v. *United States* case, the Court, I believe, recognized that . . . the children were entitled the exclusive jurisdiction of the juvenile court and its attending protections." Green was concerned that the Supreme Court might destroy the separate justice system for juveniles, which had spared children from harsh treatment in the criminal justice system.

Fortas did not buy this argument. Emphasizing the "murky facts" of *Gault*, he stated,

> One of the questions here is very simply put. If this boy was sent away for the three incidents that have been here mentioned, the baseball glove incident, whatever that was, the pocket book incident, whatever that was, and the present incident, what is there in juvenile court theory or philosophy, what is there in the theory of the juvenile court which makes it undesirable or impossible for this boy to have had the basic elements of a trial, with respect to those incidents, so that at least he would have known and we would know, the reviewing court would know, exactly what these incidents were? What happened, why was this boy sent away for six years? Is it your position that doing that would destroy the juvenile court theory?

Green explained that he believed in due process in juvenile court, but, like Parks, he had difficulty explaining to Fortas why the specific safeguards raised by *Gault* were troublesome. Ultimately, Green replied, "Well, constitutional protection applies when a person is charged with a crime." If the Supreme Court were going to apply due process cases such as *Gideon* and *Miranda* to juvenile court, "then we are going to have to say that delinquency is just another name for crime and therefore all the constitutional guarantees . . . that have been outlined today should apply." Fortas, a legal realist, dismissed this semantic argument. Much as Dorsen wanted to set aside the conceptual problem of defining *parens patriae* to focus instead on the issues in play, Fortas stated,

> I don't get anywhere by trying to solve this problem in terms of the use of a word like *crime* or *not a crime*. The question is that we are dealing here with proceedings in which persons may be deprived of liberty and put in a place for 24 hours a day, they're in custody. You can call it a crime or you can call it a horse, they are still deprived of liberty.

Ultimately, Green was unable to help Parks advance Arizona's position. Green pleaded with Fortas to remember that there is a "difference between children and adults." Fortas agreed, "Well, I think that there is a difference, just as there is a difference between a man and a woman." Finally, a couple of justices asked Green whether the National Council of Juvenile Court Judges agreed with the Ohio Association of Juvenile Court Judges and why the national association had not participated in the case. He could not answer either question definitively.

Dorsen used his reserved time to address the issue of "Gerald Gault's alleged admissions." After reviewing the relevant statements of the four witnesses (Mrs. Gault, Mr. Gault, Officer Flagg, and Judge McGhee) during the habeas corpus hearing, Dorsen concluded, "It does not sound to me like Gerald Gault specifically admitted to making those statements." He thus ended his oral argument by not only pointing out that Gerald Gault had been denied due process of law but also suggesting that he was innocent. Dorsen had performed brilliantly in his first oral argument before the Supreme Court.

The next day, Dorsen wrote to Justine Wise Polier, a well-known New York family court judge who had assisted with the case. "As you know," he reported, "the argument was yesterday. I think it went well, but more detached observers than I will have to give you the full report. One thing I do know is that Justice Fortas certainly was up on the case. He was very helpful during oral argument." Neither Parks nor Green had been able to provide satisfactory answers to Fortas's close questioning about why the specific due process protections raised by *Gault* would undermine the theory of the juvenile court.

Dorsen later learned that Chief Justice Earl Warren had assigned Fortas to write *Gault*. With his *Kent* opinion, Fortas had provided the framework for the *Gault* litigation. And, as his questioning during oral arguments demonstrated, he was the obvious choice to write the majority opinion. Like so many prominent figures in the history of American juvenile justice and the smaller universe of the *Gault* case, Fortas was Jewish. Living as a Jew in a predominantly Protestant nation partly explained why Fortas, like Charles Bernstein and Traute Maizner, identified with outsiders and gravitated toward issues that concerned those who were excluded from American constitutional protections. Even though Fortas, who was born in Memphis in 1910, had become the consummate Washington insider by the 1960s, he still empathized with outsiders.

His biographer Laura Kalman has pointed out, "Of all his opinions, *In re Gault* . . . best illustrates Fortas's personal approach to judging and his identification with those left out of society." As evidence, she highlights a 1969 speech that Fortas delivered on the case. He explained, "When we talk about juvenile offenders . . . we're talking about *all* children; our children, White as well as Black, Middle class as well as poor—not just *theirs*." Although Fortas believed that the juvenile court system was "the most appalling and dangerous part of the bankrupt estate of our national services," he could now at least ensure that juveniles received procedural due process.

Just as Dorsen had to carefully navigate the incorporation debate to avoid losing justices' votes, Fortas also had to craft his opinion carefully. Fortas discarded the initial opinion drafted by his clerk John Griffiths. Calling it "rubbish," Fortas rewrote it and began a process of revision that lasted from January until mid-May. Significantly, much of his opinion would use the Fourteenth Amendment's due process clause and conceptions of fundamental fairness to grant children constitutional rights, not the relevant provisions in the Bill of Rights. For example, although the rights to notice, confrontation and cross-examination, and counsel are all part of the Sixth Amendment, Fortas described them only as elements of generic due process. By contrast, however, he would rely explicitly on the Fifth Amendment as the source for establishing the privilege against self-incrimination in juvenile court.

His biggest challenge was to convince at least four justices to join him in attaching the privilege against self-incrimination, a foundational principle of the adversarial system of justice, to all juvenile court proceedings. At the justices' initial conference to discuss the case, even Warren and

Brennan (two of the five-vote majority in *Miranda*) did not support doing so. They may have been reluctant to do so because Dorsen and Rezneck had not asked the justices to use *Gault* to go this far. Instead, they had asked the court to guarantee this privilege only in states that allowed for the possibility of criminal prosecution of minors for their admissions in juvenile court proceedings.

Fortas, who was the most adamant proponent of the privilege against self-incrimination on the Warren Court, urged the court to extend this privilege, regardless of whether a child could be prosecuted later in a criminal court. From his perspective, juvenile courts sent children to institutions that were prisons. To keep the innocent out of such places, children required the same safeguards as adults.

Fortas reminded his brethren of their decision in the 1948 case of *Haley v. Ohio*, which involved a fifteen-year-old African American accused of murder, whom the police had arrested at midnight. Teams of police officers had questioned him until 5:00 A.M., when he confessed. His confession was later used against him and led to his conviction. For the Supreme Court, Justice Douglas, who had been Fortas's law professor at Yale and friend since the 1930s, had written this:

> What transpired would make us pause for careful inquiry if a mature man were involved. And when, as here, a mere child—as easy victim of the law—is before us, special care in scrutinizing the record must be used. Age 15 is a tender and difficult age for a boy of any race. He cannot be judged by the more exacting standards of maturity. That which would leave a man cold and unimpressed can overawe and overwhelm a lad in his early teens. This is the period of great instability which the crisis of adolescence produces. A 15-year-old lad, questioned through the dead of night by relays of police, is a ready victim of the inquisition. Mature men possibly might stand the ordeal from midnight to 5 A.M. But we cannot believe that a lad of tender years is a match for the police in such a contest. He needs counsel and support if he is not to become the victim first of fear, then of panic. He needs someone on whom to lean lest the overpowering presence of the law, as he knows it, crush him. No friend stood at the side of this 15-year-old boy as the police, working in relays, questioned him hour after hour, from midnight until dawn. No lawyer stood guard to make sure that the police

went so far and no farther, to see to it that they stopped short of the point where he became the victim of coercion. No counsel or friend was called during the critical hours of questioning.

The Court had held that the questioning of Haley had violated his due process rights and vacated his conviction.

More recently, in *Gallegos v. Colorado* (1962), the Court used *Haley* as a precedent to overturn a juvenile's murder conviction. The fourteen-year-old boy had initially confessed to the police that he had assaulted and robbed an elderly man in a hotel. Two weeks later, a juvenile court judge committed Gallegos to the State Industrial School on an indeterminate sentence. After his victim subsequently died, Colorado then prosecuted Gallegos for murder in criminal court, relying on his written confession to the police. Writing for the Court, Douglas declared,

> The youth of the petitioner, the long detention, the failure to send for his parents, the failure immediately to bring him before the judge of the Juvenile Court, the failure to see to it that he had the advice of a lawyer or a friend—all these combine to make us conclude that the formal confession on which this conviction may have rested was obtained in violation of due process.

The problem that Fortas faced, however, was that *Haley* and *Gallegos* both involved criminal prosecutions, not juvenile proceedings.

As Fortas understood, to attach the privilege against self-incrimination to all juvenile proceedings would turn *parens patriae* on its head. Instead of the state standing over the child like a parent, this privilege placed the child and the state on a level playing field. To convince Warren and Brennan why this change was necessary, Fortas circulated the recent opinion of Judge Proctor in *In the Interests of Carlo and Stasilowicz* and also a ruling by D.C. Juvenile Court Judge Orman Ketcham. In both cases, the jurists had made the point that young people were more susceptible than adults to confessing guilt to police officers. Thus, minors actually required this privilege even more so than adults. Otherwise, innocent children and adolescents would confess to crimes they had not committed.

Yet, as Fortas conceded in his final version of *Gault*, the differences between children and adults complicated building the privilege against self-incrimination into the nation's juvenile court, especially in light of *Miranda*. That decision had raised questions about whether one could waive the privilege without counsel present. As Fortas explained in *Gault*, "We appreciate that special problems may arise with respect to waiver of the privilege by or on behalf of children, and that there may well be some differences in technique—but not in principle—depending upon the age of the child and the presence and competence of parents." He added, "The participation of counsel will, of course, assist the police, Juvenile Courts and appellate tribunals in administering the privilege." Time, of course, would tell.

In his drafts of *Gault*, Fortas grouped the privilege against self-incrimination with the rights of confrontation and cross-examination. Collectively, these three due process protections were the ones most likely to change the culture of juvenile court and make it more similar to the adult adversarial system. He still needed the votes of Brennan and Warren. On March 7, Brennan sent a memo to Fortas: "This is a really magnificent opinion and I am honored to join it." Ten days later, on March 17, Warren sent Fortas a brief note. It stated: "I join your magnificent opinion in the above case. It will be known as the Magna Carta for juveniles."

Ultimately, Fortas secured six votes (Warren, Black, Douglas, Clark, Brennan, and himself) for these due process protections. It is not surprising that Fortas received the fewest votes for requiring these safeguards; they threatened to transform juvenile justice. In comparison, eight justices supported the procedural requirements most compatible with the *parens patriae* ideal: providing timely notice of charges and right to counsel. Only Potter Stewart objected to *Gault* on the principle that the juvenile court was not a criminal court and dissented. Thus, he did not vote for attaching any criminal due process protections to juvenile court.

Because the Supreme Court had not held that the federal Constitution required appellate courts or the right to appellate review, the *Gault* court did not rule on this issue. The court also did not hold that juvenile courts had to provide a transcript but suggested that the failure to record the proceedings burdened the review process, creating the need to "reconstruct a record."

Thus, his *Gault* opinion, which Fortas tinkered with until mid-May, reversed the judgment of the Arizona Supreme Court. Eight justices agreed that juvenile courts must provide notice and assistance of counsel; six supported the privilege against self-incrimination and the rights to confrontation and cross-examination of witnesses. Once *Gault* was announced, these procedural protections would become the constitutionally required law of the land for adjudicatory hearings in juvenile court. The Supreme Court, however, said that the Constitution did not mandate either a recorded transcript or appellate review.

The most remarkable features of Fortas's exceptionally long opinion were his statement of the facts and his use of social science. Like Dorsen, Fortas spent long hours refining his narrative of the case. In his description of the lewd phone call, for example, Fortas settled on the following description: "It will suffice for purposes of this opinion to say that the remarks or questions put to her were of the irritatingly offensive, adolescent, sex variety." This language cast Gerald Gault as a typical adolescent boy who had acted like one. It was his misfortune, as Fortas told Gerald's constitutional story, to appear before an incompetent judge, who sentenced him to the Arizona Industrial School "for the period of his minority [that is, until 21], unless sooner discharged by due process of law." Even though Parks had explained that Gerald had already left the school, Fortas left this fact out. Instead, he marshaled other facts from the official record to present an unsettling story of what could happen to any child in a juvenile proceeding without adequate constitutional safeguards.

Fortas incorporated social science, including drawing from the recently released *Report by the President's Commission on Law Enforcement and the Administration of Justice*, to condemn the modern juvenile court as ineffective and ill-equipped. He also used a lengthy note in the *Harvard Law Review*, "Rights and Rehabilitation in the Juvenile Courts," to drive home this point. The authors found, for example, that "between eighty and ninety percent [of juvenile courts] have no available psychologist or psychiatrist." Fortas also cited the National Council of Juvenile Court Judges' directory. It revealed that "the number of Juvenile Judges as of 1964 is listed as 2,987, of whom 213 are full-time Juvenile Court Judges." He added ominously, "half of these judges have no undergraduate degree, a fifth have no college education at all, a fifth are not members of the bar, and three-quarters devote less than one-quarter of their time to juvenile matters."

Fortas believed that these findings explained why the benevolent Progressive Era rhetoric of the juvenile court should no longer shield it from constitutional scrutiny. He explained, "Neither sentiment nor folklore should cause us to shut our eyes, for example, to such startling findings as that reported in an exceptionally reliable study of repeaters or recidivism conducted by the Stanford Research Institute for the President's

Commission on Crime in the District of Columbia." The institute researchers found that in 1966, "approximately 66 percent of the 16- and 17-year-old juveniles referred to the court by the Youth Aid Division had been before the court previously." The high rate of recidivism "could not lead us to conclude that the absence of constitutional protections reduces crime" or "that the juvenile system, functioning free of constitutional inhibitions as it has largely done, is effective to reduce crime or rehabilitate offenders." Thus, "the features of the juvenile system which its proponents have asserted are of unique benefit will not be impaired by constitutional domestication."

He also cited the work of the applied sociologists Stanton Wheeler and Leonard Cottrell of the Russell Sage Foundation, who had studied the effects of the juvenile justice system on adolescents. They found that "when the procedural laxness of the 'parens patriae' attitude is followed by stern disciplining, the contrast may have an adverse effect upon the child, who feels that he has been deceived or enticed." This sense of betrayal was especially true for children who were sent to industrial schools. As Fortas explained, the description of these prisons as schools was euphemistic. The reality for the inmate was that "instead of mother and father and sisters and brothers and friends and classmates, his world is peopled by guards, custodians, state employees, and 'delinquents' confined with him for anything from waywardness to rape and homicide."

The fact that children could be imprisoned for being found delinquent set the stage for Fortas's most famous statement in *Gault*. "[I]t would be extraordinary if our Constitution did not require the procedural regularity and the exercise of care implied in the phrase 'due process.' Under our Constitution, the condition of being a boy does not justify a kangaroo court." He added, "The traditional ideas of Juvenile Court procedure, indeed, contemplated that time would be available and care would be used to establish precisely what the juvenile did and why he did it—was it a prank of adolescence or a brutal act threatening serious consequences to himself or society unless corrected?" In other words, Gerald Gault could be sentenced to serve a potential six-year prison sentence for a prank phone call, and his cellmate might be a rapist or murderer.

Fortas, like Dorsen, laid out first the detailed facts of the case (Section I), followed by a critique of the state of modern juvenile justice (Section II), before he addressed the procedural due process protections required in an adjudicatory hearing in juvenile court. "Notice of Charges" (Section

III) and "Right to Counsel" (IV) were short because there was already so much consensus on these two issues. "Confrontation, Self-Incrimination, and Cross Examination" (Section V) was longer because Fortas had had to convince his colleagues that the facts of *Gault* had raised these issues and that the Supreme Court should use the *Gault* case to extend these safeguards to juvenile court. He also included extended discussions of the recent opinions by Justice Proctor and Judge Ketcham to support his argument about the danger of false confessions. Finally, "Appellate Review and Transcript of Proceedings" (Section VI) was only a couple of paragraphs because the court held that these provisions did not apply to juvenile court.

Three weeks before the Supreme Court officially delivered its decision in *Gault*, Fortas visited Syracuse University to dedicate the Arnold M. Grant Auditorium at its law school and receive an honorary degree. His speech described how liberals from the New Deal to the Great Society had transformed American law and society. "We have crossed the threshold of a new world—whether we like it or not. We have created a vast new assortment of legal rights—rights to welfare benefits of various sorts; rights to medical care, to pensions, to unemployment compensation; rights against employers; rights to vote; rights to equal treatment." He explained that these changes were the product of "the revolutionary yeast in our society," "the powerful turmoil and movement of our own society," and the "worldwide upsurge of the demands that heretofore quiescent people are making upon their own societies."

Without specifically mentioning *Gault*, he used sections of his forthcoming opinion to respond to the critics who blamed the Supreme Court for the nation's crime wave. Fortas began, "There are those who say that the Constitution and the Supreme Court are coddling criminals—that we are sacrificing the rights of society in the interests of the criminals among us." He explained that "we must insist upon maintaining the guarantees of our Constitution, generously construed and applied," but also contended that the Supreme Court was not responsible for rising crime rates. "The sharpest evidence of the fallacy of this attack," he explained,

> can be found in comparing the figures as to adult crime with those registering offense committed by juveniles. In all except one or two jurisdictions under the American Flag—the exception, I'm glad to say including New York—none of these constitutional principles [i.e.,

the Warren Court's due process decisions] has been applied to juveniles, a term which generally includes persons under 18 years of age or younger.

Instead, states treated juveniles "as constitutional nonpersons and heretofore outside of the scope of the Supreme Court interpretations of the constitutional principles." Thus, "the police arrest them and interrogate and search them with abandon, and there is evidence that they did so. They could obtain confessions without the *Miranda* warnings, and they did so. Juveniles could be and were tried without the benefit of appointed counsel. Generally, they couldn't appeal, so that the Supreme Court's decisions did not stand in the path of eliminating crime." Yet "the nonapplication of the Constitution's principles has not eliminated juvenile offenses or slowed down their rate." From 1960 to 1965, he pointed out, the juvenile crime rate increased more than the adult rate. Moreover, in 1965, "Juveniles accounted for one-fifth of arrests for serious crimes of all kinds."

After defending the due process revolution, Fortas concluded,

> Freedom's advance has always been assailed. People always fear freedom, and each step along the road to fulfillment of its promise is hotly contested. But I have no doubt that, with care and prudence, our progress will continue; and in this progress, law and lawyers will be called upon to play a leading role. I am confident that we will prove worthy of this high calling.

He envisioned that lawyers in juvenile court would be part of that future.

On May 15, 1967, from his seat on the bench in the Supreme Court, Fortas read excerpts from his nearly sixty-page *Gault* opinion. It was an 8–1 decision. Justices Black and White wrote brief concurrences; Harlan wrote a longer opinion concurring in part and dissenting in part. Only Stewart dissented. As expected, Black used his concurrence to argue for the theory of total incorporation that would apply "the specifically and unequivocally granted provisions of the Fifth and Sixth Amendments" to juvenile court proceedings and condemned Harlan's "fundamental fairness" approach. Harlan used his concurrence to respond to Black. He defended fundamental fairness and applied it to juvenile justice. Using this approach, Harlan contended that timely notice, assistance of counsel, and a written record were the only procedural requirements necessary in juvenile court. He did not believe that the Constitution required extending the privilege against self-incrimination or the right to confrontation and cross-examination of witnesses. These requirements, in his opinion, would "radically alter the character of juvenile court proceedings."

White, who had dissented from the majority in *Miranda*, was closer to Harlan's position. He did not think that the court should have reached the issue of the privilege against self-incrimination because "there was not an adequate basis in the record for determining whether that privilege was violated in this case." He also noted that Gerald Gault had been found delinquent in 1964, "long before the *Miranda* decision," so his case "was a poor vehicle for resolving a difficult problem." For somewhat similar reasons, White explained, "I would not reach the questions of confrontation and cross-examination."

Potter Stewart was the lone dissenter. He argued that it was "sadly unwise as a matter of judicial policy" for the court "to use an obscure Arizona case as a vehicle to impose upon thousands of juvenile courts throughout the Nation restrictions that the Constitution made applicable to adversary criminal trials." Stewart, who was from Cincinnati, Ohio, agreed with the Ohio Juvenile Judges Association that juvenile courts were different from criminal courts. "The object of the one is correction of a condition. The object of the other is conviction and punishment for a criminal act." He predicted that "to impose the Court's long catalog of requirements upon juvenile proceedings in every area of the country is to invite a long step backwards into the nineteenth century. In that era, there were no juvenile proceedings, and a child was tried in a conventional criminal court with all the trappings of a conventional criminal trial." He added, "So it was that a 12-year-old boy named James Guild was tried in New Jersey for killing Catharine Beakes. A jury found him guilty of murder, and he was sentenced to death by hanging. The sentence was executed. It was all very constitutional."

After learning about the court's decision, Roger Baldwin sent his "qualified congratulations" to Dorsen. Dorsen thanked him and acknowledged Baldwin's concerns about what would happen to children after they were found delinquent. Dorsen noted, "I agree that it is important that judges continue to have wide discretion after a finding of delinquency. I also believe that there is much much more work to be done in the area of treatment (or punishment), and I hope that this decision will clear the way for expenditure of resources in that direction." In response to another friend's congratulations, Dorsen wrote, "Yes, Gault was a famous victory, and I only hope that the revolution turns out to be a benign one—which it will be if effort is expended on improving the pre-adjudicative and treatment aspect of the juvenile court system."

Fortas was also proud of *Gault* and sent friends and supporters autographed copies of the opinion. In a letter to Elizabeth Wickenden, he stated, "First, I want to thank you very much for your marvelous letter about the *Gault* case. I have sent Mrs. Gertrude Mainzer an autographed copy of the *Gault* opinion. I am sure you realize that I don't ordinarily just send around autographed copies of opinions. My favorite ego outlet is my violin." Wickenden also shared with Fortas a letter from Dame Eileen Younghusband, a pioneering English social worker who had served as the Chairman of the Hammersmith (London) Juvenile Court. Younghusband offered her perspective on the case. She explained,

> The original affair in the Arizona Juvenile Court seemed to me quite horrifying and the judge's decision out of all proportion to the seriousness of the offense—if indeed an offence was committed at all. I reflected with some amusement that here the curious charge in such cases is: stealing electricity, value 2d, from the Postmaster General—since all that can be proved is that the boy made a call, not that the obscene conversation took place. In such cases we should usually levy a small fine or else discharge the boy conditionally, i.e., he could be further dealt with for the original offense if he committed a further offence within the ensuing year.

Thus, the London judge recommendations included the same punishment that the Gault family had expected from Judge McGhee on the fateful day that he sentenced Gerald to Fort Grant.

On May 27, 1967, the Council of Judges of the National Council on Crime and Delinquency unanimously passed a resolution supporting the *Gault* decision and distancing itself from what had happened in Arizona. The resolution stated that the Supreme Court decision "reaffirms the standards for juvenile and family courts developed over many years by the Council of Judges of the National Council on Crime and Delinquency, the National Council of Juvenile Court Judges, and the United States Children's Bureau." They added, "Basically, *Gault* reiterates that juvenile and family courts are courts of law, and not social welfare agencies" and "We do not read the *Gault* decision as undermining the non-criminal character of juvenile and family courts, or as abrogating their judicial concepts, whose intrinsic soundness was affirmed by the justices even though they were compelled to view them through the unsympathetic and atypical lens shaped from the facts of the *Gault* case." Judge Ketcham, whose ruling on the unreliability of juvenile confessions had helped Fortas to win the necessary votes for attaching the privilege against self-incrimination to juvenile proceedings, mailed the resolution to Fortas. Fortas happily wrote back: "This is cheering!"

Fortas also sent a signed copy of *Gault* to Dorsen. Dorsen was completing his book *Frontiers of Civil Liberties,* which would include his briefs in Supreme Court cases such as *Gideon* and *Gault.* Dorsen had not known what the *Gault* decision would look like, who would write it, or when the Court would issue it. In a letter to his publisher, Dorsen explained, "Frankly, I think there is a good chance that the Court will reverse the decision below—that is, hold for the appellant, at least in part. What will be the tenor of the opinion is anyone's guess, but I would be surprised if the Court failed at least to rule that a right to counsel exists in delinquency hearings." He added, "The decision should be handed down by the end of June unless the case is set down for re-argument next fall. In that event, there probably will be no decision until early 1968. In view of past experience the overwhelming likelihood is that the case will not be reargued."

After Dorsen read all the opinions in *Gault,* he wrote to Fortas. "I may be prejudiced," he observed, "but if the decision is indeed a landmark, it will largely be due to the comprehensive and careful way in which you dealt with the issues." He added, "The 'thanks' you so generously gave me is much appreciated, but it is really I and my colleagues who owe thanks to you for laying the groundwork in the Kent case as well as for your opinion in Gault." Dorsen and Rezneck would spend the summer writing a law review article analyzing the unresolved due process issues in juvenile court, such as a right to a jury trial. They were already working on Act Two in the constitutional domestication of American juvenile justice.

Supporters of the decision, who considered it an extension of *Gideon,* now spoke about Dorsen and Fortas in the same breath. For example, Melvin Karpatkin, who served as interim legal director of the ACLU in 1967, proclaimed that "the principal congratulations should go to Professor Norman Dorsen of New York University School of Law, and also a Vice-Chairman of the Board of Directors of the ACLU, who was the principal draftsman of the brief. Undoubtedly many contributed to the splendid result achieved in this case. But for me, the two whose names should be remembered when the history of the Gault case will be written are those of Justice Fortas and Professor Dorsen."

Not to be forgotten, Amelia Lewis wrote to the ACLU Board. She explained, "As a member from Arizona may I express to our national Board my appreciation for the assistance and encouragement given me by Mel Wulf and Board member Norman Dorsen in connection with my court battle for Gerald Francis Gault, which, through their fine advices to me and argument in court, resulted so successfully in the decision announced by the Supreme Court yesterday." Dorsen responded immediately: "It is we who owe you our thanks. Although there may be glory in arguing before the Supreme Court, it was due largely if not entirely to your efforts that the case got that far. So the Gaults and other families should honor you for your good work." He added, "I am delighted that the reaction in Arizona has been swift and apparently not unfavorable."

Because the Supreme Court had ordered Arizona to pay $697.80 to cover the clerk's costs and to print the record, Lewis continued her work on the case. After Gila County refused to pay, she had to negotiate with the governor's office to have the state legislature pass a special bill in 1968 to reimburse the ACLU. Lewis also battled with Arizona to expunge Jerry's juvenile conviction from his record. Jerry had been officially released from the custody of the Arizona Industrial School for Boys on January 26, 1967, but he would not be eligible to enlist in the army unless his record was cleared.

When the Supreme Court announced its decision, Jerry was seventeen years old and enrolled in a training program studying welding at the Job Corps Center in Pleasanton, California. He learned about the decision from a local reporter. Over the years, he would have more to say about what had happened to him.

Opponents of the *Gault* decision viewed it as a mistaken extension of *Miranda*. *The New York Daily News* ran an editorial with the headline, "Now, the Juveniles." The editors were dismayed that the Supreme Court had taken the due process revolution to the juvenile court. They argued that the court had chosen "perhaps the worst time in our national experience to throw its bombshell. Juvenile crime currently is at its highest recorded rate, and rising." Instead, the paper suggested that "if the court had decided along lines of greater discipline, then its 'new law' might have been welcomed as an aid in the efforts to solve the problem. But the court did just the opposite. It made it tougher for the police and courts to handle youthful violators."

Along similar lines, the chairman of civic affairs for the United Business Men's Association of Great Philadelphia wrote to Fortas to express his members' dismay. "As I understand it now if a Juvenile is caught in the act of breaking and entering—he can refuse to make a statement—he must be furnished with an attorney—then he can be released in bail [*sic*] to continue his handiwork until his case comes up—which may take a year." He wanted to know whether "in laymans [*sic*] language as described above—is this correct? If so then let me congratulate you for complete protection and misplaced sympathy for the Juvenile Offender." He added, "Perhaps in the community that you work and live in you do not come into contact with the violence that has caused our citizens to stay off the streets after dark—drive with locked car doors—make jails out of their homes and business with bars and barbed wire. How do we get the Supreme Court to consider our position and our rights?"

Such frustrations would have consequences for the Supreme Court and juvenile justice in the coming years.

Just Deserts

CHAPTER 5

"*Kent* and *Gault* Already Seem like Period Pieces"

On May 15, 1967, the same day that the U.S. Supreme Court announced its *Gault* decision, CBS broadcast to an international audience a "town meeting of the world," in which New York's Democratic senator Robert F. Kennedy debated California's new Republican governor Ronald Reagan on the topic, "The Image of America and the Youth of the World." College students from Africa, Asia, and Europe, who were attending British universities, questioned Kennedy and Reagan about American foreign policy via a satellite feed from a BBC studio in London. Anna Ford, a British student, set the tone for this trans-Atlantic interrogation. She began, "I believe the war in Vietnam is illegal, immoral, politically unjustifiable, and economically motivated." These college students represented the New Left and its scathing critique of American foreign policy and contempt for those liberals who represented the establishment.

Fifteen million Americans watched Kennedy and Reagan defend American Cold War foreign policy. Kennedy was visibly uncomfortable. He apologized repeatedly for mistakes made by his brother's administration and emphasized what now needed to be done. By contrast, Reagan, who during his gubernatorial campaign recommended harnessing "the youthful energy [of juvenile delinquents] with a strap," stood up to the students and demonstrated a strong command of foreign policy. His conservative boosters were elated with his performance, and commentators credited Reagan with winning the debate. Afterwards, Kennedy told his aides never to put him on the same stage again with "that son-of-a-bitch." Many, however, assumed that the debate was a preview for a future presidential contest between these standard bearers of liberalism and conservatism.

By May 1967, the Vietnam War was undermining the Great Society and shattering the New Deal coalition that had elected Democratic presidents from Franklin Roosevelt to Lyndon Johnson. On April 4, 1967, for instance, Martin Luther King, Jr., had condemned the war in his address "Beyond Vietnam," delivered at the Riverside Church in New York City. King proclaimed that "a nation that continues year after year to spend more money on military defense than on programs of social uplift is approaching spiritual death." This unraveling of liberalism as the nation's dominant political philosophy at the end of 1960s had profound consequences for American constitutional law and juvenile justice.

In the spring of 1967, the editors of the recently launched *Family Law Quarterly* invited Norman Dorsen and Daniel Renzeck to contribute an article on the future of juvenile law. Dorsen and Reznneck explained that "predicting the future development of the law in the wake of *In re Gault* is a risky business. The case represented the Supreme Court's first foray into the no-man's land of federal constitutional rights of juveniles, but it will obviously not be the last." They added, "So far-reaching a decision will initiate a lengthy process of constitutional adjudication, accompanied by legislative change and alteration of administrative and judicial practices." They emphasized that change would mostly take place at the state level and added that the "Supreme Court can be expected to participate only sporadically in this process of change, through the review of cases carefully selected to focus on critical problems of the juvenile system." They surmised that "the Supreme Court's role therefore may consist primarily of formulating basic minimal procedural standards for the conduct of juvenile justice, without undertaking to frame a detailed code of juvenile procedures."

The future of American juvenile justice thus depended partially on how the Supreme Court decided to apply *Gault* as a precedent. Although some court watchers believed that *Gault* would inevitably lead to the Supreme Court's requiring juvenile courts to follow the same due process procedures as criminal courts, Dorsen and Reznneck disagreed. They explained that the Court had explicitly rejected arguments, based on the Fourteenth Amendment's equal protection clause, that children and adults had to be treated similarly in all circumstances. Although they had a difficult time deciphering the ambiguous underlying rationale of the majority opinion in *Gault*, they concluded that Fortas's opinion exemplified Justice Brennan's selective incorporation method that the Court was using to nationalize criminal procedure. They also made the perceptive point that the Court would not mandate specific safeguards for juvenile courts until they had applied the particular provision to state criminal courts. They did not, however, anticipate that the Supreme Court would use juvenile justice cases initially to expand and later restrict the rights of adults in criminal courts.

As a starting point for their predictions, Dorsen and Rezneck explicated the Court's precise holdings in *Gault* before surveying how much constitutional terrain remained uncharted. They explained that the Court had "divided juvenile proceedings into three phases—prejudicial, adjudicative, and dispositional—and emphasized that its holdings were directed only to the adjudicative stage." The only due process rights that *Gault* had guaranteed were the right of the juvenile and his or her parents or guardian to receive both written notice of charges and advice of the right to the assistance of counsel, the privilege against self-incrimination, and the requirement that witnesses must testify under oath and be available for confrontation and cross-examination.

The *Gault* court had explicitly reserved five significant questions about adjudicatory hearings:

(a) Whether, and to what extent, the juvenile court may admit hearsay or other testimony normally inadmissible under the rules of evidence.
(b) What the correct burden of proof is in such a proceeding.
(c) Whether there is a right to have a transcript or other record kept of the proceedings.
(d) Whether there is a right to appeal from an adjudication of delinquency in such a proceeding.
(e) Whether a juvenile court judge must state the grounds for his finding when he is the trier of fact.

The court had also remained silent on three "major procedural questions relating to the conduct of adjudicative hearings." These were "the right to a trial by jury, the right to a public proceeding, and the right of compulsory process to secure witnesses for the defense." Clearly, *Gault* had only begun the constitutional domestication of the juvenile court.

They also noted the Court had completely avoided ruling on any issues relating to either the pre-judicial stage or the dispositional phase. It would have been unrealistic to expect the justices to have done so because, as Dorsen and Rezneck wrote, the Court avoids questions "not necessary for decision or inadequately developed in the record below." Thus, the justices had chosen not to consider many critical issues. Were juveniles "entitled to invoke the constitutional guarantee against unreasonable searches and seizures?" Did they have "rights to bail, a hearing to test the legality of pre-hearing detention, and other safeguards against unlawful confinement?" Were "pre-hearing statements made by juveniles to police or probation officers" in custody "governed by the requirements of *Miranda v. Arizona?*" Did juvenile court judges have the power "to determine the adequacy of treatment being received by a committed juvenile?" This final issue, of course, had been central to the Fort Grant scandal of 1952.

Dorsen and Rezneck also explained that the Court had softened the impact of the due process revolution. The Court made newly incorporated procedural rights prospective, instead of retrospective. This meant that the Supreme Court required states to implement these procedural protections only for future cases. Therefore, states did not have to re-adjudicate cases decided before the Supreme Court had ruled on the issue. They predicted correctly that "although *Gault* itself is silent on the point, the same prospective application will probably be accorded to most, if not all, of the rights newly recognized in *Gault* and to those which may be applied in future cases."

Dorsen and Rezneck argued that the path of the law after *Gault* depended on how fast and how far the Supreme Court selectively incorporated provisions from the Bill of Rights into the Fourteenth Amendment's due process clause. They pointed out, for example, that "the Sixth Amendment right to trial by jury has not yet been held to be fully incorporated into the Fourteenth Amendment and therefore applicable in state criminal trials." Unless it was applied to state criminal courts, they doubted that the Court would require this procedural protection for juvenile courts. They were also unsure whether the Court, if it used the selective incorporation method, would consider the right to a jury trial "essential to a fair trial in juvenile court."

In analyzing jury trials, Dorsen and Rezneck also made an important distinction between requiring them in delinquency cases based on the violation of the criminal law and those involving petty or status offenses. Juvenile status offenses are acts that are wrongful only because the offender is a minor. The latter cases, they believed, were not suited for jury determination. Drawing the distinction between how to handle "kids' stuff" and combat "true crime" became a major focus of juvenile justice policy in the 1960s and 1970s. President Johnson's Commission on Law Enforcement's Task Force on Juvenile Delinquency and Youth Crime, for example, envisioned that juvenile courts would eventually separate petty and status offenders from those juveniles who committed serious offenses. The former, they believed, should have their cases handled without formal intervention. The latter, however, should be handled in a formal system that had most of the trappings of a criminal court. States such as New York revised their juvenile laws to create new classifications, such as Person In Need of Supervision (PINS), to distinguish between minors who were status offenders and "delinquents" who had committed criminal offenses.

Decriminalizing status offenders, in fact, became an essential feature of the 1974 Justice Juvenile and Delinquency Prevention Act. This federal law required states to develop plans to stop incarcerating noncriminal offenders. Failure to comply would cost states their eligibility for federal block grants. As a result, by the end of the twentieth century, the cases of status offenders dropped to approximately 15 percent of the juvenile court's caseload. Status offenders were also institutionalized much less frequently than they had been earlier in the twentieth century. The overall drop in the number of status offender cases, however, masked how girls' cases were handled, including the use of private facilities to incarcerate them.

Dorsen and Rezneck strongly believed that the Supreme Court would require juvenile courts in cases involving criminal offenses to follow the same standard for proof—"beyond a reasonable doubt"—criminal courts used. They explained that *Gault*'s "rejection of the 'civil' label as a justification for differing procedures in the juvenile court should be a red flag as to procedures imported from civil cases, such as the preponderance of the evidence test." They believed that *Gault* would operate against using a civil standard in juvenile cases, "even though the Supreme Court has never held that the reasonable doubt standard is constitutionally required in state criminal cases." Moreover, "While the antecedents and development of the concept are uncertain, and it does not appear in the Bill of Rights, long usage in every jurisdiction has firmly implanted the standard as proof of every element of a criminal offense." They supported this development because

the reasonable doubt standard impresses on the trier of fact the ne-
cessity of reaching a subjective state of certitude of the facts in issue;
the preponderance test is susceptible to the misinterpretation that its
calls on the trier of fact merely to perform an abstract weighing of the
evidence in order to determine which side has produced the greater
quantum, without regard to its effect in convincing his mind of the
truth of the proposition asserted.

Thus, Dorsen and Rezneck counted on the Supreme Court to recognize
the evolution of the criminal law. In light of this history, they argued that
it was "difficult to see how the distinctive objectives of the juvenile court
give rise to a legitimate institutional interest in finding a juvenile to have
committed a violation of the criminal law on less evidence than if he were
an adult."

Tellingly, Dorsen and Rezneck ended their article with a short section
on the "right to treatment." They noted that "the judicial storm-signals
are flying that the special handling of juveniles through the juvenile court
process can be validated in the long run only if a concentrated assault is
made on a major national problem: the poverty of community resources
devoted to the realization of rehabilitative goals." They quoted a passage
from the 1967 report on the Task Force on Juvenile Delinquency and
Youth Crime, which lamented, "the community's continued unwillingness
to provide the resources—the people and facilities and concern necessary
for individualized treatment." They concluded, "The Court is impatient
with the rhetoric and determined to confront the realities of the process."
For them, "the real promise of the decision lies in the responsibility and
opportunity it affords all who are concerned with problems of the juvenile court to do likewise."

As their final section revealed, Dorsen and Rezneck read *Gault* in the
context of the Warren Court's due process revolution and President Johnson's Great Society agenda. They did not know that both the Warren
Court and the Great Society would soon be historical artifacts.

Amelia Lewis and Lorna Lockwood, whose involvement was critical to
the early stages of the *Gault* litigation, also worked to shape the meaning
of the decision in Arizona and the nation. Both participated in conferences sponsored by the Institute of Continuing Legal Education, serving
on panels whose transcripts were published in *Gault: What Now for the Juvenile Court?* As Lewis explained, "I will leave reading *between* the lines to

the law professors. This is one of the reasons why I am happy to be here. I am going to find out what my decision means, just as you are finding out." She added, "I believe, on the basis of this decision and the *Miranda* decision, that every juvenile who is in court for the purpose of a hearing which may result in his incarceration, must have full rights, including full rights of counsel at all times. This will be my position on any case that I will handle in the future." She added,

> As a matter of fact, this has been the position of the juvenile judge of Maricopa County, Arizona, ever since he received a copy of my brief. He immediately sent out word to the local Bar association that we were all on a list to represent juveniles without compensation. He was not going to have any case overruled in the event that by some chance I succeeded in *Gault*.

For her contributions to juvenile law, in 1987 the American Bar Association awarded Lewis the prestigious Livingston Hall Juvenile Justice award.

Lockwood also agreed with much of Fortas's *Gault* decision but added, "I cannot admit that the Arizona court which precipitated the *Gault* case was run as badly as the Supreme Court opinion assumes." She believed "the lawyers of our land are interested, and feel at last the juvenile court will become a real part of the judicial system, instead of a social agency with unlimited power but which has not as yet been able to justify itself as a vehicle for justice as well as mercy." As a former juvenile court judge, she also stressed that juvenile courts could help their local communities address the root causes of delinquency instead of relying solely on the police to arrest offenders after the fact. Thus, Lewis and Lockwood also believed that the future of juvenile justice rested primarily in the hands of local communities and the states but expected the Supreme Court to clarify many of constitutional issues left unanswered in *Gault*.

The Institute of Continuing Legal Education panels in New York City; Ann Arbor, Michigan; and Boulder, Colorado; also previewed a new, revisionist understanding of the history of juvenile justice. Unlike legal liberals who had gone to great lengths during the *Gault* litigation to speak approvingly of the benevolence of the founders of the juvenile court, a young English sociologist, Anthony Platt, challenged this interpretation. He was completing a book manuscript, *The Child Savers: The Invention of Delinquency,* that accused progressives such as Julian Mack and Jane

Addams of developing the juvenile court as a middle-class instrument of social control to wield against the working class. Platt was helping to run a neighborhood legal clinic in Chicago, with the eminent criminologist Norval Morris.

Morris, who was born in New Zealand, had served as founding director of the United Nations Institute for the Prevention of Crime and Treatment of Offenders from 1962 to 1964 before joining the law faculty of the University of Chicago. He praised Platt's forthcoming book, which Morris described as sketching the "origins of the juvenile court, and in particular, the juvenile court of Cook County." According to Morris, Platt had revealed that the juvenile court had "emerged from what I suppose everybody agrees was a legal misinterpretation of the *parens patriae* concept." He explained,

> Though we keep on prating *parens patriae,* we might as well burn incense. Historical idiosyncrasies gave us a doubtful assumption of power over children. With the quasi-legal concept of *parens patriae* to brace it, this assumption of power blended well with the earlier humanitarian traditions in the churches and other charitable organizations regarding child care and child saving. Being somewhat facetious about it, the juvenile court is thus the product of paternal error and maternal generosity, which is a not unusual genesis of illegitimacy.

He added,

> In 1899, then, the juvenile court of Cook County was born. Its siblings multiplied rapidly throughout the world, with their procedural informality, inquisitorial as distinct from adversarial systems of justice, their surprising power to control the lives of children who had not committed a crime, but who were neglected and in need of care and protection, as well as children who were incorrigible, who were truants, etc. All of such courts were equipped with a vast rhetoric of benevolence.

Much like the college students who challenged Kennedy and Reagan and condemned the nation's foreign policy, scholars Platt and Morris questioned the legitimacy of American juvenile justice. *The Child Savers* became a canonical text in the field.

History was also made on Monday, October 2, 1967, when the Supreme Court convened its first term since *Gault* had been decided. President Johnson came to watch his former solicitor general Thurgood Marshall swear the judicial oath "to administer justice without respect to persons, and do equal right to the poor and the rich" and become the 96th justice of the nation's high court. Marshall, the great-grandson of a slave, who had successfully litigated *Brown v. Board of Education,* had become the nation's first African American justice. He replaced Tom Clark, who had retired so that his son Ramsey Clark could become attorney general of the United States. Marshall, it turned out, was the final justice nominated by Johnson to be confirmed by the Senate, and the final member of the Warren Court.

The next year, 1968, marked a turning point in American history. The historian Arthur Schlesinger, Jr., who had served as a special assistant to President Kennedy and President Johnson before becoming the Albert Schweitzer professor of humanities at the City University of New York, lamented that the nation had lost its way. In his view, Americans had begun the 1960s with great expectations but now faced a crisis of confidence. The assassinations of Martin Luther King, Jr., on April 4 and then Robert Kennedy on June 5 were tragic evidence of this state of affairs. As Schlesinger explained, "One after another—John F. Kennedy, Martin Luther King, Jr., Robert F. Kennedy—fell before assassin's bullets. Why should not the young despair about such a society?"

Eight days after Robert Kennedy's death, Chief Justice Earl Warren, who was seventy-seven years old, sent a short note to President Johnson:

My dear Mr. President:

Pursuant to the provisions of 28 U.S.C. Section 371 (b), I hearby advise you of my intention to retire as Chief Justice of the United States, effective at your pleasure.

Warren wanted Johnson, not Republican Richard Nixon, to nominate his successor. As the journalists Bob Woodward and Scott Armstrong explained, the Nixon campaign had taken aim at the Warren Court: "Throughout the 1968 presidential campaign, Nixon had run against Warren and his Court as much as he had run against his Democratic rival, Hubert Humphrey. Playing on prejudice and rage, particularly in the South, he promised that his appointees to the Supreme Court would be different." Warren believed that a jurist like Fortas, who shared his vision of legal liberalism, should lead the Court and wanted to keep Nixon, whom he despised, from having the opportunity to choose his successor.

By June 1968, President Johnson, however, was already a lame duck.

On March 31, 1968, in a surprise televised address to the nation, Johnson announced that he would neither seek nor accept his party's nomination for the presidency. As a result, he had lost what remained of his diminishing political capital. The President nominated Fortas to become Chief Justice. Fortas, who had remained one of Johnson's closest advisors on domestic and foreign policy matters even while serving on the Supreme Court, appeared to be a logical choice. Johnson explained that he decided to nominate Fortas because he "was the most experienced, compassionate, articulate, and intelligent lawyer I knew, and because I was certain that he would carry on in the Court's liberal tradition." He also nominated the federal judge Homer Thornberry, a former Texas congressman, to take the seat that Fortas would vacate if he were promoted. Thus, the justice who had written the court's two juvenile court decisions was poised to become chief justice.

Clark Clifford, an advisor to Democratic presidents since Harry Truman, told Johnson that he should have nominated Fortas and Thornberry before he had made his March announcement. As he told Johnson, "you can't get it through now because the Republicans are planning on winning in November of '68." He added, "One of the best things that could happen for this country would be for Abe Fortas to be chief justice, but you're never going to get it through." Still, Johnson tried.

After extensive and contentious hearings, the Senate Judiciary Committee had voted 11-to-6 to support Fortas's confirmation, but freshman Senator Robert Griffin of Michigan led a Republican filibuster that ultimately convinced Fortas in October to ask President Johnson to withdraw his nomination. Conservative Democrats, who shared Republican displeasure with the Warren Court's due process revolution, had refused to vote for cloture to end the filibuster and effectively doomed Fortas's nomination. This meant that President Nixon, not Johnson, would select Warren's successor.

The Nixon Administration then pressured Fortas to resign from the Supreme Court. On May 11, 1969, *Life* magazine reported that Fortas in 1966 had accepted a $20,000 retainer from the family foundation run by Louis Wolfson. Fortas's fellow justices were stunned to learn from him that this was an annual retainer. At the time, Wolfson was being investigated for stock fraud and would later go to prison. Two days later, Fortas told his colleagues that he was retiring. Thus, in 1969, both Warren and

Fortas departed from the Supreme Court. They had cast decisive votes in the most controversial 5–4 due process decisions.

On May 21, 1969, Nixon nominated Warren Burger, a judge on the D.C. circuit of appeals who had criticized the morality of the Supreme Court's *Miranda* decision, to become chief justice. After the Senate confirmed him in a 74-to-3 vote, Burger was sworn into office by Warren and became the nation's fifteenth chief justice. He presided over the Supreme Court from 1969 to 1986. His court did not overturn the Warren Court's controversial due process decisions, such as *Miranda*, but did instead develop exceptions to these standards of due process and limited appellate review of criminal cases. The Burger Court allowed the due process revolution in criminal justice to stand but worked to limit its impact.

Although the nomination and confirmation of Burger went smoothly, Nixon ran into trouble when he tried to appoint a conservative white Southerner to replace Fortas. He hoped to use the appointment as part of his "southern strategy" to undercut Southern support for George Wallace in the 1972 election and to transform the traditionally Democratic South into a stronghold of the modern Republican Party. The Nixon Administration tried to eviscerate the Voting Rights Act of 1965, which was up for renewal in 1970s. It also adopted a passive policy, known as "benign neglect," toward African Americans. The southern strategy played on white hostility to the civil rights movements and replaced the explicit racial epithets used by segregationists in the 1950s and early 1960s with racially coded language about crime. George Wallace had developed this new political vocabulary, and Richard Nixon learned to speak it fluently.

Yet Nixon misread the mood of the U.S. Senate. The Senate first rejected Judge Clement Haynsworth, Jr., a South Carolinian who served on the U.S. Court of Appeals for the Fourth Circuit. Nixon then nominated G. Harold Carswell, a Georgian and white supremacist, who had recently been confirmed to a judgeship on the U.S. Court of Appeals for the Fifth Circuit. Carswell quickly ran into trouble. Famously, Senator Roman Hruska of Nebraska declared, "Even if he is mediocre, there are a lot of mediocre judges and people and lawyers, and they are entitled to a little representation, aren't they?" The Senate voted down Carswell's nomination, although the vote was close: 51 to 45.

On January 20, 1970, the Burger Court, which lacked a replacement for Fortas, heard its first juvenile justice case, *In re Winship*. The case was significant because it was the first application of *Gault*. The issue in *Winship* involved the proper constitutional standard of proof judges must use during adjudicatory hearings, one that the Court had reserved in *Gault*. Just as Dorsen and Rezneck had predicted, the Supreme Court used *Gault* as a precedent to determine that juveniles were entitled to be judged on the standard of reasonable doubt.

In *Winship*, New York City family court judge Millard Midonick used the less stringent "preponderance of the evidence" standard required by the New York Family Court Act to find twelve-year-old Samuel Winship delinquent. Winship had been accused of stealing $112 from a woman's pocketbook in a locker room. The judge stated, as part of the case's official record, that if he had been required to use the reasonable-doubt standard, he would not have been able to reach this result. During the subsequent dispositional hearing, Midonick committed Winship for eighteen months to a training school, "subject to annual extension of his commitment until his 18th birthday." Thus, Winship, like Gerald Gault, could be incarcerated for six years because he was declared a delinquent. Winship appealed his conviction on the grounds that the Constitution required that juvenile courts use the reasonable-doubt standard. The New York Court of Appeals rejected this argument and affirmed the juvenile court's ruling.

On January 23, 1970, the eight members of the Burger Court met to discuss *Winship*. William Douglas kept careful notes on these judicial conferences, in which the chief justice speaks first, followed by the associate justices in order of seniority. Each justice explains his or her position on the case, including how he or she will vote. Douglas recorded Burger's analysis of *Winship*: "The only issue is the weight of the evidence. We could have all criminal trials by preponderance of evidence. I do not see the constitutional question. Every step the Court has taken in [the] juvenile field has been toward the abolition of juvenile courts." He added that he would vote to affirm the decision of the New York Court of Appeals. Thus, unlike Warren, who considered Fortas's opinion in *Gault* to be the Magna Carta for juveniles, Burger did not support *Gault*.

Hugo Black, the senior associate justice, spoke next. Because of his theory of total incorporation, Black had supported *Gault*'s application of provisions from the Fourth and Fifth Amendments to juvenile court adjudicatory hearings. Yet he distinguished *Winship* from *Gault* because the Bill of Rights contained no explicit language about standards of proof. Thus, he did not believe that *Winship* raised a federal question. Five members of the Burger court, however, believed that juvenile courts were constitutionally required to use the standard of reasonable doubt. In order of seniority, they were Douglas, John Marshall Harlan, William Brennan, Byron White, and Thurgood Marshall. Marshall, the final justice to join the Warren Court, cast the decisive fifth vote on the Burger Court to extend *Gault*. Speaking last, he explained, "[Winship] was charged with a crime, or at least a form of a crime. 'Person' in the Bill of Rights includes juveniles."

Since the chief justice was not in the majority, it fell to Douglas, the senior majority justice, to select the author for the Court's majority opinion. Douglas chose Brennan to pick up in *Winship* where Fortas had left off in *Gault*. As Brennan declared in conference, "After *Gault*, we can't retreat." Yet it was going to be difficult for Brennan to craft an opinion that held together the five justices who supported requiring reasonable doubt. The problem was that the justices took divergent paths to reach this conclusion and differed over how broad the decision should be.

Brennan thus had to find the middle ground that could hold together the fragile majority. Douglas, for example, believed that juveniles were constitutionally entitled to the same procedural due process as adults. He did not want *Winship* to declare otherwise, especially at a time in the nation's history when 40 percent of Americans were minors. Accordingly, Brennan had to remove the following language from his opinion:

> We recognize that the 'condition of being a boy' may have a bearing on the nature of the due process to which a child is entitled. As a result of their youth, children are generally less responsible for their conduct than adults, just as they are more in need of guidance and more susceptible to its influence. In order to serve their special needs and to take advantage of their special abilities, the juvenile process appropriately differs from the criminal process in many respects. The possibility exists, accordingly, that the 'denial of rights available to an adult may be offset, mitigated, or explained by action of the Government, as *parens patriae*, evidencing solicitude for the juveniles.

As critics of the Supreme Court's juvenile justice decisions in *Gault* and *Winship* have pointed out, the Court's decisions elided this important idea that children were developmentally different from adults.

Whereas Douglas had made Brennan cleanse his opinion of *parens patriae*, Harlan insisted that *Winship* be written narrowly. To keep Harlan's vote, Brennan had to explain that the decision applied only to juveniles charged with a criminal offense. Under New York law, juvenile courts also had jurisdiction over "persons in need of supervision." Harlan did not want *Winship* to cover these noncriminal cases and wrote a concurring opinion to elaborate his position. Brennan did not mention noncriminal cases explicitly in his opinion. Instead, he incorporated the distinction into his specific framing of the issue in *Winship*. He stated at the outset, "This case presents the single, narrow question whether proof beyond a reasonable doubt is among the 'essentials of due process and fair treatment' required during the adjudicatory stage when a juvenile *is charged with an act which would constitute a crime if committed by an adult*" (italics added).

Harlan also insisted that the Court's decision should not imply that children had a right to jury trials in juvenile court. To retain Harlan's vote, Brennan made no mention of jury trials and eliminated from his opinion an explicit discussion of the balancing test that the Supreme Court would use to determine which due process protections could be incorporated into the juvenile court without destroying its unique mission.

After defining the issue in the case narrowly, Brennan's opinion then traced the history of the rise of the reasonable-doubt standard from the beginning of U.S. history to Dorsen's and Rezneck's 1967 article predicting that the Supreme Court would determine that juvenile courts must also follow this standard. Brennan explained,

> It is critical that the moral force of the criminal law not be diluted by a standard of proof that leaves people in doubt whether innocent men are being condemned. It is also important in our free society that every individual going about his ordinary affairs have confidence that his government cannot adjudge him guilty of a criminal offense without convincing a proper fact finder of his guilt without utmost certainty.

Brennan had used *Winship* to announce for the first time that the reasonable-doubt standard was constitutionally required in criminal courts. To put this issue to rest, he explained, "Lest there remain any doubt about the constitutional stature of the reasonable-doubt standard, we explicitly hold that the Due Process Clause protects the accused against conviction except upon proof beyond a reasonable doubt of every fact necessary to constitute the crime with which he is charged." After Brennan made this pronouncement, he then turned to the question of "whether juveniles, like adults, are constitutionally entitled to proof beyond a reasonable doubt when they are charged with violation of a criminal law." The answer, of course, was a resounding yes, but only for five justices.

Whereas Black dissented because of the absence of textual language in the Bill of Rights about standards, Burger, like Stewart, believed that juvenile courts were not criminal courts. Burger wrote a dissent that Stewart joined, and made his opposition to *Gault*-like decisions absolutely clear.

> Since I see no constitutional requirement of due process sufficient to overcome the legislative judgment of the States in this area, I dissent from further strait-jacketing of an already overly restricted system. What the juvenile court system needs is not more, but less, of the trappings of legal procedure and judicial formalism; the juvenile court system requires breathing room and flexibility in order to survive, if it can survive, the repeated assaults from this Court.

He added that *Winship*, like *Kent* and *Gault*, "is really a protest against inadequate juvenile court staffs and facilities; we 'burn down the stable to get rid of mice.'" Burger cautioned against transforming juvenile courts into criminal courts. He concluded, "I cannot regard it as a manifestation of progress to transform juvenile courts into criminal courts, which is what we are well on the way to accomplishing. We can only hope the legislative response will not reflect our own by having these courts abolished."

In *Winship*, the Burger Court, by a 5–3 vote, had built cautiously and narrowly on *Gault* to continue the constitutional domestication of the juvenile court. The Court's personnel, however, would change again before it heard another juvenile justice case.

After two defeats, Nixon gave up on placing a conservative Southerner on the court and instead nominated U.S. Court of Appeals for the Eighth Circuit Judge Harry Blackmun, a boyhood friend of Burger's from St. Paul, Minnesota, to fill the vacancy. On May 12, 1970, the Senate voted 94-to-0 to confirm Blackmun. Burger and Blackmun, dubbed the "Minnesota Twins," provided the necessary votes to end the due process revolution. Initially, they voted together on criminal cases but later parted ways on many constitutional questions. Unexpectedly, Blackmun became one of the most liberal justices in the history of the Supreme Court. For example, he wrote the majority opinion in the abortion rights case *Roe v. Wade* (1973) and became a leading opponent of the constitutionality of the death penalty.

As it turned out, Blackmun, the newest justice, wrote the plurality opinion in *McKeiver v. Pennsylvania*. The issue on appeal was whether the due process clause of the Fourteenth Amendment required a trial by jury in the adjudicative phase of a juvenile court hearing. In *McKeiver,* like *Brown v. Board of Education,* the Supreme Court consolidated several cases from different states that addressed the same constitutional question. *McKeiver* combined two cases from Pennsylvania that involved criminal offenses committed by minors. In 1968, sixteen-year-old Joseph McKeiver had been charged with robbery, larceny, and receiving stolen goods. As Blackmun noted, "McKeiver's offense was his participating with 20 or 30 youths who pursued three young teenagers and took 25 cents from them." He added, "McKeiver never before had been arrested and had a record of gainful employment." Fifteen-year-old Edward Terry had a more troubled past, including being institutionalized. In this case, he had been charged with assault and battery on a police officer and conspiracy. The week before, Terry had also assaulted a teacher. Both McKeiver and Terry requested jury trials, but their requests were denied by the juvenile court.

Although McKeiver and Terry had been charged with serious offenses that would have been considered crimes if they were adults, the Supreme Court combined their cases with forty-six others from North Carolina that involved black children, ranging in age from eleven to fifteen years old. These North Carolina cases supplied confirmation of the findings of the U.S. Civil Rights Commission that some Southern communities used their juvenile courts against the civil rights movement. Fortas had incorporated an abbreviated version of Dorsen's long footnote in his *Gault* brief into a footnote of his own in *Gault* but had not addressed this issue squarely in the text of his opinion.

In 1968, the forty-six African American children from Hyde County, North Carolina, had protested "schools assignments and a school consolidation plan." With adult protestors, the children marched along "Highway 64 singing, shouting, clapping, and playing basketball." North Carolina state highway patrolmen filed delinquency petitions against the children, charging them with "willfully impeding traffic." One child was also charged with making "riotous noise" and rearranging the furniture in a principal's office. The same lawyer represented all of the children, requesting jury trials for each one, and objected to the judge's decision to exclude the general public from witnessing all but two of the cases. The juvenile court judge declared all the children to be delinquent because they had committed "an act for which an adult may be punished by law." He committed them to the County Department of Public Welfare for incarceration "until such time as the Board of Juvenile Correction or the Superintendent of said institution may determine, not inconsistent with the laws of the State." The judge then suspended the commitments and placed all the children on one to two years of probation on the condition that they violate no state law, report monthly to the County Department of Welfare, be at home every night before 11:00 P.M., and attend a school approved by the County Welfare Director. This coercive ruling seemed to confirm Anthony Platt's damning history of the juvenile court as an instrument of social control.

Blackmun began the *McKeiver* opinion with a doctrinal recitation of the Supreme Court's cases addressing juvenile defendants from *Haley v. Ohio* (1948) to the recently decided *Winship*. He used this review to emphasize that the Supreme Court had never declared that juvenile courts were identical to criminal courts and to deny that it intended to destroy the juvenile court. He then reviewed the facts of the Pennsylvania and North Carolina cases before turning to whether jury trials were required in juvenile court. Surprisingly, he asserted, "All the litigants here agree that the applicable due process standard in juvenile proceedings, as developed by *Gault* and *Winship*, is fundamental fairness." Blackmun had subtly shifted the court's approach to juvenile justice cases. Instead of using the selective incorporation method, he applied Harlan's preferred and more restrictive approach. Using the "fundamental fairness" test, Blackmun concluded that "a trial by jury is not constitutionally required in the adjudicative phase of a state juvenile court delinquency proceeding."

Blackmun also restored *parens patriae* to juvenile justice jurisprudence. He explained, "The juvenile concept held high promise. We are reluctant to say that, despite disappointments of grave dimensions, it still does not hold promise, and we are particularly reluctant to say, as do the Pennsylvania appellants here, that the system cannot accomplish its rehabilitative goals." He added,

So much depends on the availability, on the interest and commitment of the public, on willingness to learn, and on understanding as to cause and effect and cure. In this field, as in so many others, one perhaps learns best by doing. We are reluctant to disallow the States to experiment further and to seek in new and different ways the elusive answers to the problems of the young, and we feel that we would be impeding that experimentation by imposing the jury trial.

Blackmun's language sounded more like Justice Charles Bernstein's opinion for the Arizona Supreme Court in *Gault* than Fortas's opinion for the U.S. Supreme Court.

Combining the Pennsylvania and North Carolina cases, which arguably raised different issues because the Keystone state allowed the public to attend juvenile court hearings and the Tar Heel state did not, led to a plurality opinion. Only Burger, Stewart, and White joined Blackmun's opinion, although Harlan concurred in both judgments. Brennan wrote a separate opinion to concur in the judgment in the Pennsylvania case but dissented from the judgment in the North Carolina case. Brennan believed that allowing the public to witness juvenile court proceedings provided similar protections to a jury trial and thus found that the Pennsylvania system provided a fair trial. The North Carolina system, in his opinion, did not. Thus, there were only five votes for one of the two judgments in *McKeiever*.

Douglas wrote a dissenting opinion, joined by Black and Marshall, arguing for the continuation of the constitutional domestication of the juvenile court. He stated: "[W]here a State uses its juvenile court proceedings to prosecute a juvenile for a criminal act and to order 'confinement' until the child reaches 21 years of age, or, where the child, at the threshold of the proceedings, faces that prospect, then he is entitled to the same procedural protection as an adult." He quoted liberally from *Kent* and *Gault* to drive home this point that juveniles facing possible long-term incarceration were constitutionally entitled to the same procedural due process rights as adults. Unlike Blackmun, who resuscitated *parens patriae*, Douglas's opinion read more like Fortas's opinions that condemned juvenile justice as "the worst of both worlds."

Within a few years, Fortas's opinions would be treated as relics. Only a decade after *Gault* had been decided, the Brookings Institution published Donald Horowitz's *Courts and Social Policy*. In his account of the unintended consequences of court-ordered reform, Horowitz wrote,

> More than most opinions of the Warren Court, *Kent* and *Gault* already seem like period pieces. Authored by Mr. Justice Fortas, the opinions are suffused with the meliorism of the mid-1960s. This was, after all, the time of the great programs and the great commissions: the Crime Commission, the Civil Disorders Commission, the Campus Unrest Commission, the Violence Commission. It was a time when the nation

was being told that sharp precipices lay ahead unless the country turned onto other roads, and a time when a number of such turns were taken.

He added, "In general, the *Kent* and *Gault* opinions share this perspective—that things are wrong, but not so wrong that they cannot be righted if the problems are faced squarely."

Drawing on studies of the administration of juvenile justice in the wake of *Gault*, Horowitz concluded, "Although juvenile court judges and lawyers place a premium on compliance with law and the procedural basis of justice, they also entertain a number of other beliefs about the best way to handle juveniles in trouble, these beliefs seriously qualifying their commitment to the adversary process for juveniles." Thus, "the tenacity of these beliefs led them to seek ways of adapting *Gault*, rather than pursuing the decision to its ultimate implications." For example, as Anthony Platt had explained to the Institute of Continuing Legal Education audiences in 1968,

> If you sit around the Cook County Juvenile Court in Chicago long enough, you hear the judges say the following when a defendant comes before the court: "You have a right to counsel. If you do not have counsel, we can appoint counsel for you, but on the other hand that would mean going away and coming back another day. Therefore, if you feel that you want to save time and go ahead with it now, I will hear it now."

Empirical studies also revealed only partial compliance with *Gault*. Norman Lefstein, Vaughan Stapleton and Lee Teitelbaum, for example, studied three urban courts before and after *Gault*. They found that judges in one of the court systems did not inform juveniles of their right to counsel. The second court system informed only 3 percent of the juveniles of this constitutional right, and the third system informed them in 56 percent of the cases. Judges in these courts also rarely informed juveniles of their right to confront the witnesses against them and the privilege against self-incrimination. Studies of rural courts also revealed that judges rarely followed the court's *Gault* opinion. Twenty year later, in his article "*In re Gault* Revised," Barry Feld found similarly disturbing levels of non-compliance. More recently, Feld has documented that many states still do not appoint counsel for juveniles.

The tenacity of localism in American legal history, coupled with officials' beliefs about how to best serve their own communities, largely explains the reluctance to implement nationally mandated standards for the administration of juvenile justice. In addition, because the Supreme Court stopped short of requiring jury trials or appellate review in juvenile court, judges, such as Robert McGhee in Globe, Arizona, retained control over their courtrooms. After *Gault,* for example, McGhee continued to win reelection to the bench.

McKeiver halted the constitutional domestication of the juvenile court, leaving it as a Progressive Era institution retrofitted with only some basic due process protections. Instead of focusing on the functional similarities between juvenile and criminal courts as Fortas had done in *Gault,* the Burger Court used *parens patriae* to emphasize their differences as a justification for not requiring additional procedural protections. States could largely decide how to run their juvenile courts, and judges could adapt *Gault,* instead of adapting to *Gault.*

In 1971, the year that *McKeiver* was decided, the personnel of the Burger Court also changed. Due to serious health issues, both Black and Harlan resigned and died shortly thereafter. Nixon nominated sixty-four-year-old Lewis Powell, a moderate Southerner and former president of the American Bar Association, to replace Black, who had been the lone Southerner on the Court. The same day that the president nominated Powell, he also nominated forty-seven-year-old William Rehnquist to replace Harlan. Rehnquist, a former law clerk to Justice Robert Jackson, was the assistant attorney general in charge of the Office of Legal Counsel, which advises the executive branch on constitutional issues. Rehnquist, the smart Arizona conservative about whom Dorsen and Ares had corresponded during the *Gault* litigation, was the more controversial choice. Although Powell and Rehnquist were both confirmed, Rehnquist received the most "no" votes of any successful nominee for the Court up to that time in its history.

Powell and Rehnquist joined the Burger Court on January 7, 1972. Powell became a swing vote, and Rehnquist was its youngest and most conservative member. Because he wrote so many solo dissenting opinions, he became known as the "Lone Ranger." Time, however, was on his side. In 1986, Ronald Reagan, who was serving his second term as President, nominated him to become chief justice. After the Senate confirmed him

65-to-33, he became the sixteenth chief justice and served until his death in 2005.

Reagan also nominated Arizonan Sandra Day O'Connor in 1981 to become the first woman justice of the Supreme Court. The Senate unanimously confirmed her. O'Connor had been a classmate of Rehnquist at Stanford Law School. He graduated first in their class; she graduated third. O'Connor also took the Arizona Bar Examination on the same day as Amelia Lewis. They were the only two women to do so. O'Connor, like Lorna Lockwood, blazed a trail in Arizona politics. O'Connor served as the chairperson of the Maricopa County Juvenile Detention Home Visiting Board from 1963 to 1965. She then became assistant attorney general of Arizona. She later served in the Arizona legislature, becoming the first woman elected Arizona senate majority leader. She left politics for the bench in 1975, winning election to the Maricopa County Superior Court. Governor Bruce Babbitt later appointed her to the Arizona Court of Appeals.

The two Arizonans, O'Connor and Rehnquist, played a prominent role in the final juvenile justice case decided by the Burger Court. The 1984 case, *Schall v. Martin,* originated in New York City and addressed the constitutionality of a law that allowed for the pretrial detention of accused juvenile delinquents due to a "serious risk" that they would commit another crime before their hearing. A federal district court judge struck down the New York law, and the New York Court of Appeals upheld this ruling because the majority of juveniles who had been detained subsequently had their cases dismissed or were released after being adjudicated delinquent. The court concluded that children detained before trial were being unlawfully punished.

Rehnquist believed that this was a simple case because "the charge of the denial of due process is simply frivolous." O'Connor, who had overseen the Phoenix juvenile court detention center, considered it a harder case, but, like Rehnquist, considered the preventive detention law constitutional. At the justices' conference, she explained, "This type of statute is prevalent in most states and, if we throw it out, we create a serious situation. What the statute requires [notice, a hearing, and a statement of facts and reasons], while slim, is enough to avoid constitutional difficulty." She added, "I'd allow more of this for juveniles than adults." She cast the decisive vote at the conference. Chief Justice Burger assigned Rehnquist to write the majority decision.

In his opinion, Rehnquist tersely summarized the facts of Martin's case. "Appellee Gregory Martin was arrested on December 13, 1977, and charged with first-degree robbery, second-degree assault, and criminal possession of a weapon based on an incident in which he, with two others, allegedly hit a youth on the head with a loaded gun and stole his jacket and sneakers." He added, "Martin had possession of the gun when he was arrested. He was 14 years old at the time and, therefore, came within the jurisdiction of New York's Family Court. The incident occurred at 11:30 at night, and Martin lied to the police about where and with whom he lived. He was consequently detained overnight." He similarly described the serious charges against the other teenagers.

Rehnquist believed that this was a straightforward case because since *McKeiver* the Court used the fundamental fairness test in juvenile justice cases. The question was whether preventive detention was compatible with fundamental fairness. Rehnquist explained that there were only two questions to be resolved. One was whether there were enough procedural protections to ensure a fair process. Because the New York law provided some protections, including a hearing, Rehnquist believed it constituted due process. The bulk of his opinion addressed the second question: "Does preventive detention under the New York statute serve a legitimate state objective?" Citing *De Veau v. Braisted,* a 1960 Supreme Court case that predated the due process revolution, Rehnquist answered the question: "The 'legitimate and compelling state interest' in protecting the community from crime cannot be doubted." He added, "The harm suffered by the victim of a crime is not dependent upon the age of the perpetrator," and cited a FBI report on juvenile violent crime. Although Rehnquist's statement about age in this context supported his argument about why juveniles were a threat to public safety, three years later, in *United States v. Salerno,* Chief Justice Rehnquist relied on *Schall* to uphold the constitutionality of an adult pretrial-detention statute. Unlike Brennan, who had used a juvenile justice case in 1970 to require the reasonable-doubt standard to be used in the nation's criminal courts, in 1987 Rehnquist used a juvenile justice case to restrict the due process rights of adults in criminal court.

In *Martin,* Rehnquist used *parens patriae* to define incarceration as a legitimate expression of state authority. He noted that the statute allowed for only seventeen days of detention and that this confinement should not be considered punishment. He explained,

The conditions of confinement also appear to reflect the regulatory purposes relied upon by the State. When a juvenile is remanded after his initial appearance, he cannot, absent exceptional circumstances, be sent to a prison or lockup where he would be exposed to adult criminals. Instead, the child is screened by an "assessment unit" of the Department of Juvenile Justice. The assessment unit places the child in either nonsecure or secure detention. Nonsecure detention involves an open facility in the community, a sort of "halfway house," without locks, bars, or security officers where the child receives schooling and counseling and has access to recreational facilities.

Rehnquist also reasoned that the secure detention was "consistent with the regulatory and *parens patriae* objectives relied upon by the State. Children are assigned to separate dorms based on age, size, and behavior. They wear street clothes provided by the institution and partake in educational and recreational programs and counseling sessions run by trained social workers. Misbehavior is punished by confinement to one's room." Thus, "We cannot conclude from this record that the controlled environment briefly imposed by the State on juveniles in secure pretrial detention 'is imposed for the purpose of punishment,' rather than as 'an incident of some other legitimate governmental purpose.'" Defenders of Fort Grant in the 1950s, in an era when Rehnquist himself moved to Arizona, had made similar arguments that it was an industrial school, not a prison.

Once a lone dissenter, Rehnquist now wrote for a six-member majority, concluding his opinion with an attack on the spirit of legal liberalism that had animated the decisions of the late Warren and early Burger courts:

> The dissent would apparently have us strike down New York's preventive detention statute on two grounds: first, because the preventive detention of juveniles constitutes poor public policy, with the balance of harms outweighing any positive benefits either to society or to the juveniles themselves, and, second, because the statute could have been better drafted to improve the quality of the decision-making process. But it is worth recalling that we are neither a legislature charged with formulating public policy nor an American Bar Association committee charged with drafting a model statute.

Marshall dissented, joined by Brennan and John Paul Stevens. Stevens, a Gerald Ford appointee, had joined the Burger Court in 1975 and eventually became the most outspoken liberal voice on the Roberts Court (2005–) until his retirement in 2010. His successor, Elena Kagan, nominated by Barack Obama, had served as a law clerk for Marshall in the late 1980s and later became solicitor general.

It was ironic that in 1984 two justices from the state of Arizona determined that New York's pretrial incarceration policy was not punishment, especially since twenty years earlier New York City lawyers had been so instrumental in convincing the Supreme Court to condemn desert justice in Arizona.

During the period from 1964 to 1984, two remarkable changes had occurred in American law and society. First, Rehnquist's brand of constitutionalism had become ascendant. Second, Americans unexpectedly embraced mass incarceration as a penal strategy. In the 1960s, experts who questioned the ability of the criminal justice system to rehabilitate offenders had imagined that the nation's incarceration rate would remain the same or perhaps decline. From 1929 to 1964, the rate of incarceration in the United States had fluctuated around 100 prisoners per 100,000 people. It stayed at this level until the early 1970s, and then began to decline. Criminologists such as Norval Morris predicted that the nation would move away from imprisonment as a penal strategy.

Instead, the opposite happened. By the time that Ronald Reagan was elected president in 1980, the nation had fully embraced mass imprisonment, and the nation's incarceration rate would nearly quintuple by 2006. Initially, the juvenile justice system spared many children and adolescents from the "get tough" approach. As Franklin Zimring has shown, during the 1970s and 1980s, "the diversionary objective of the juvenile justice insulated delinquents from the brunt of a high magnitude expansion in incarceration in the criminal justice system." The success of diverting youth from the criminal justice system helps to explain why in the 1990s the juvenile court became a target for "get tough" proponents. The punitive turn in American juvenile law, which included transferring younger adolescents to criminal court, raised troubling questions about differential handling of cases based on race and ethnicity, the competency of younger adolescents to stand trial, the related issue of the culpability of adolescent offenders for their offenses, and the economic costs and effectiveness of prosecuting juveniles as adult offenders.

The "get tough" era for adults and children, as Michael Tonry, a scholar of law and criminology, has explained, meant that Americans supported punishing their fellow citizens in ways that were "unimaginable in most other Western countries," such as permitting "capital punishment, sentences for life without the possibility of parole, mandatory minimum sentences measured in decades, and the prosecution of children as if they were adults." These harsh practices, known to juvenile justice experts as "just deserts," led scholars to mine American history and culture to explain the widening divide between American and European approaches to criminal punishment. Perhaps they needed only to visit Arizona.

Epilogue

In 2007, more than thirty children's rights associations and law centers sponsored a "Gault at 40" campaign that included dramatic re-enactments of the oral arguments, programs to train lawyers to be juvenile defenders, and several academic conferences. The organizers of these events hoped to use the anniversary of *Gault* to bring about meaningful change. They were encouraged that the Supreme Court in *Roper v. Simmons* (2005) had declared that the Eighth and Fourteenth Amendments prohibited states from using the death penalty on offenders who were under the age of eighteen when their crimes were committed. Yet they were also discouraged about the state of juvenile justice. For example, in an article in the *Harvard Civil Rights/Civil Liberties Law Review,* the executive director of the National Juvenile Defender Center, Patricia Puritz, explained that "the promise of *In re Gault* remains largely unfulfilled and, indeed, the juvenile defense bar is in crisis. Vigorous representation on behalf of young clients is not widespread or even common, and in some juvenile courts is discouraged." She added, "Children are subject to more punitive sanctions than before, longer sentences, harsher institutional conditions, zero tolerance mandates, DNA testing, placement on lifelong sex offender registries, erosion of confidentiality protections, and decreased procedural protections related to transfer to adult court, to name a few." Also deeply troubling was the fact that "these laws have negatively impacted racial and ethnic minority youth, and have drawn large numbers of indigent children deeper into the justice system." This meant that "far too many indigent children appear in our nation's juvenile courts, defenseless and powerless against the state, and subject to consequences that carry lifelong implications of which they are unaware."

To help renew interest in juvenile justice, the sponsors of Gault at 40 invited Gerald Gault to tell his story. He was fifty-eight years old, retired from the army after twenty-three years of distinguished service to his country, and a grandfather. He repeated that he had not made any of the lewd comments in what had become the most famous phone call in American constitutional history. He also said that Fort Grant had taught him "how to be angry, to be mean," and that he spent the next thirty years trying not to be an angry, mean person. He thanked his wife—and Amelia Lewis, who had died in 1994—for saving his life. He added, "People in this society need to realize that these children that we are putting behind bars, without counsel, are our next leaders."

Norman Dorsen also contributed his reflections to Gault at 40. Dorsen, who became the ACLU's general counsel in 1969 and later its president from 1976 to 1991, still taught at New York University Law School and continued to serve as the co-director of the Arthur Garfield Hays Civil Liberties Program. He recounted the exciting *Gault* litigation and also acknowledged that "there have been enormous disappointments in terms of the implementation of *Gault*." He lamented that there was still insufficient funding for juvenile courts and too few juvenile defenders. He concluded, "So, in that sense, *Gault* has been a disappointment, but it would have been far worse if we had lost." In light of the subsequent history of American constitutional law, it is unlikely that a *Gault*-like case could have been won after 1971.

Gault was a period piece, but an important one. Although this due process decision proved impossible to implement fully because of local resistance and the unfinished constitutional domestication of the juvenile court, it did help to cement in American law the idea that children had constitutional rights. Another case involving an adolescent in an Arizona middle school, which was working its way through the legal system during *Gault's* fortieth anniversary, reminds us why this idea matters.

The case involved Savana Redding from Safford, Arizona, fewer than forty miles from Fort Grant. April Redding, Savana's mother, had sued the Safford Unified School District #1 and three school officials (Assistant Principal Kerry Wilson; Helen Romero, an administrative assistant; and Peggy Schwallier, the school nurse) for violating her daughter's Fourth Amendment right against unreasonable searches. In October 2003, the assistant principal believed that the thirteen-year-old girl was hiding prescription painkillers in her underwear. He ordered Schwallier and Romero to strip search her in the nurse's office. Wilson, Romero, and Schwallier, relying on the defense of qualified immunity, petitioned the District Court for the District of Arizona for a summary judgment. The District Court, which held that there was no Fourth Amendment violation, granted their motion and dismissed the case. A three-judge panel of justices from the Ninth Circuit Court of Appeals also found that the search strip of Redding did not violate the Fourth Amendment and affirmed the district court ruling. Ultimately, a divided circuit, sitting en banc, reversed the decision. They declared that the school officials had violated Redding's rights, and they denied the officials qualified immunity.

The school district appealed to the U.S. Supreme Court. On June 25, 2009, Justice David Souter, whom President George H. W. Bush had nominated in 1990 to replace William Brennan, delivered the majority opinion in *Safford Unified School District #1 v. Redding*. Souter had grown up in New Hampshire, graduated from Harvard University, received a Rhodes scholarship to attend Oxford University, and returned to Harvard for his law degree. Souter disappointed his conservative backers and became a liberal voice on the high court. The year after his *Safford* opinion, Souter retired. He was replaced by Sonia Sotomayor, the nation's first Latina justice.

In *Safford,* Souter stated, "The issue here is whether a 13-year-old student's Fourth Amendment right was violated when she was subjected to a search of her bra and underpants by school officials acting on reasonable suspicion that she had brought forbidden prescription and over-the-counter drugs to school." Souter concluded that the assistant principal had grounds to search Redding's outer clothing and her backpack but had then crossed a constitutional line. As he explained, "The exact label for this final step in the intrusion is not important, though strip search is a fair way to speak of it." He described what had happened in the nurse's office.

> Romero and Schwaillier directed Savana to remove her clothes down to her underwear, and then "pull out" her bra and the elastic band on her underpants. Although Romero and Schwallier stated that they did not see anything when Savana followed their instructions, we would not define strip search and its Fourth Amendment consequences in a way that would guarantee litigation about who was looking and how much was seen. The very fact of Savana's pulling her underwear away from her body in the presence of the two officials who were able to see her necessarily exposed breasts and pelvic area to some degree, and both subjective and reasonable societal expectations of personal privacy support the treatment of such a search as categorically distinct ... [from] a search of outer clothing and belongings.

Souter added, "Savana's subjective expectation of privacy against such a search is inherent in her account of it as embarrassing, frightening, and humiliating." Unlike Gerald Gault, who was expected to be seen but not heard during his own habeas corpus hearing, Savana Redding's testimony made a constitutional difference. Like Fortas, who had incorporated the findings of applied sociologists in *Gault*, Souter drew on social scientific studies to explain the psychological harm caused by strip searching school children.

Seven justices joined Souter's opinion that declared the strip search unconstitutional "because there were no reasons to suspect the drugs presented a danger or were concealed in her underwear." Seven justices, including Souter, also held that the school officials were entitled to qualified immunity from liability because the case law on school strip searches was unclear. The school officials, according to Souter's reasoning, could not have known definitely that they were violating Redding's constitutional rights. Redding thus could not sue them for damages, even though they had violated her rights.

Justice John Paul Stevens dissented from this part of Souter's opinion. Stevens stated that *Safford* was a "case in which clearly established law meets clearly outrageous conduct." As Stevens explained, including quoting from one of his earlier opinions on this issue, "It does not require a constitutional scholar to conclude that a nude search of a 13-year-old child is an invasion of constitutional rights of some magnitude."

Ruth Bader Ginsburg, who in 1993 had become the second woman to serve on the Supreme Court, joined Stevens' dissent and wrote her own. She had grown up in a Jewish family in Brooklyn, New York, during the Great Depression and later graduated from Columbia Law School. In 1972, she helped found the ACLU Women's Rights Project and had argued six sex discrimination cases before for the Burger Court, winning five of them. Like Stevens, Ginsburg objected to Assistant Principal Wilson's brand of desert justice. She believed that the search should have stopped after the "inspection of Redding's backpack and jacket pockets yielded nothing." She added,

> Wilson had no cause to suspect, based on prior experience at the school or clues in this case, that Redding had hidden pills—containing the equivalent of two Advils or one Aleve—in her underwear or body. To make matters worse, Wilson did not release Redding, to return to

class or to go home, after the search. Instead, he made her sit on a chair outside his office for over two hours. At no point did he attempt to call her parent. Abuse of authority of that order should not be shielded by official immunity.

But it was. The Court had recognized a right without granting any remedy.

Souter's majority opinion was also so factually narrow that it provided no guidance for future cases. Could school officials, for example, strip search a boy instead of a girl? Was it acceptable to strip search a seventeen-year-old rather a thirteen-year-old girl? *Redding* thus raised more questions than it answered.

Justice Clarence Thomas, like Souter, was nominated by President George H. W. Bush to replace a liberal icon on the Supreme Court. He succeeded Thurgood Marshall, becoming the second African American justice. Thomas, who was born to teenage parents in Pin Point, Georgia, had been raised by his grandfather in Savannah. He attended Catholic schools, did his undergraduate work at Holy Cross, and graduated from Yale Law School. Unlike Souter, Thomas did not disappoint conservatives. Instead, he became a leading proponent of conservative constitutionalism and an advocate for the jurisprudence of originalism. This interpretive method contends that the Constitution should be construed according to those who enacted the relevant provision in question. During the 1980s, conservative jurists and scholars popularized this method in response to the legal liberalism of the Warren and early Burger courts.

As a conservative Southerner, Thomas empathized with desert justice more than his Northern colleagues. He concurred in the Court's judgment that the school officials had qualified immunity, but dissented forcefully from the Court's ruling that these officials had violated Redding's rights. He also objected to Ginsburg's concurrence, noting that "the suggestion that requiring Redding to sit in a chair for two hours amounted to a deprivation of her constitutional rights, or that school officials are required to engage in detailed interrogations before conducting searches for drugs, only reinforces the conclusion that the Judiciary is ill-equipped to second-guess the daily decisions made by public administrators."

Thomas's opinion was similar to Potter Stewart's dissent in *Gault*. Whereas Stewart had used the *parens patriae* ideal to argue that the Supreme Court should not interfere with the juvenile court, Thomas used the common-law doctrine of *in loco parentis* in a similar fashion. He declared, "[T]he task of implementing and amending public school policies is beyond this Court's function. Parents, teachers, school administrators, local politicians, and state officials are all better suited than judges to determine the appropriate limits on searches conducted by school officials. Preservation of order, discipline, and safety in public schools is simply not the domain of the Constitution. And, common sense is not a judicial monopoly or a Constitutional imperative." He added, "The Court's interference in these matters of great concern to teachers, parents, and students illustrates why the most constitutionally sound approach to the question of applying the Fourth Amendment in local public schools would in fact be the complete restoration of the common-law doctrine of *in loco parentis.*"

To recover this lost legal world, Thomas quoted from William Blackstone's 1765 *Commentaries on the Laws of England,* an 1837 North Carolina decision, and the 1873 edition of James Kent's *Commentaries on American Law.* He advocated "a return to the understanding that existed in this Nation's first public schools, which gave teachers discretion to craft the rules needed to carry out the disciplinary responsibilities delegated to them by parents." Accordingly, he urged the Court to turn the constitutional clock back to the time before juveniles (or adults for that matter) had constitutional rights to due process of law in state courts or institutions.

Thomas added, "Restoring the common-law doctrine of *in loco parentis* would not, however, leave public schools entirely free to impose any rule they choose." He quoted extensively from his 2007 concurring opinion in the student speech/conduct case *Morse v. Frederick* (popularly known as the Bong Hits 4 Jesus case) to argue that the individual rights provisions of the Bill of Rights should not apply to schoolchildren. In *Morse,* he argued, "In my view, the history of public education suggests that the First Amendment, as originally understood, does not protect student speech in public schools." In the eighteenth and nineteenth centuries, Thomas pointed out, "Teachers commanded, and students obeyed. Teachers did not rely solely on the power of ideas to persuade; they relied on discipline to maintain order." He added, "If parents do not like the rules imposed by those schools, they can seek redress in school boards or legislatures; they can send their children to private schools or home school them; or they can simply move."

Drawing again on his *Morse* opinion, Thomas stated,

the majority has confirmed that a return to the doctrine of *in loco parentis* is required to keep the judiciary from essentially seizing control of public schools. Only then will teachers again be able to "govern the[ir] pupils, quicken the slothful, spur the indolent, restrain the impetuous, and control the stubborn" by making "rules, giv[ing] commands, and punish[ing] disobedience" without interference from judges.

He concluded, "By deciding that it is better equipped to decide what behavior should be permitted in schools, the Court has undercut student safety and undermined the authority of school administrators and local officials. Even more troubling, it has done so in a case in which the underlying response by school administrators was reasonable and justified. I cannot join this regrettable decision."

In many ways, Thomas's opinion echoed much of the testimony from many of the proponents of desert justice who appeared before the Joint Committee to Investigate the Management and Operation of the Arizona Industrial School in 1952. Whereas they distinguished whippings and forced barefoot marches from torture, he disputed whether Redding had been "strip searched" because she had not been completely naked or had her body cavities inspected. He explained, "The distinction between a strip search and the search at issue in this case may be slight, but it is a distinction that the law has drawn."

No other member of the court joined Thomas's dissent. Much as Gerald Gault's punishment for allegedly making an obscene phone call seemed disproportionate and unjust in 1964, so did the strip search of Savana Redding nearly forty years later. In both cases, it ultimately required the U.S. Supreme Court to secure justice for the child. After learning about the Supreme Court's decision, Redding, who was a college student, told reporters, "I'm pretty excited about it, because that's what I wanted." She added, "I wanted to keep it from happening to anybody else." She sounded just like Gerald Gault.

The Supreme Court, as the history of *Gault* reveals, has made constitutional promises to children but must rely on other state actors to keep them. It remains primarily in the hands of local communities to safeguard the constitutional rights of their children, whether they are in the public schools or the deep end of the juvenile justice system.

December 19, 1872	The U.S. Army establishes Fort Grant at the foot of Mount Graham. The United States government later gives Fort Grant to Arizona after the territory becomes a state.
July 3, 1899	The world's first juvenile court, located in Cook County, Illinois, hears its first case.
February 14, 1912	Arizona becomes the 48th state.
March 29, 1913	Arizona establishes an Industrial School at Fort Grant.
January 23, 1949	Gerald Francis Gault is born.
June 1, 1950	John Schapps and Milton Rector begin their study of Fort Grant.
Early January 1952	Phillip Pierce is released from Fort Grant and travels to Phoenix to tell Judge Charles Bernstein about abuses occurring at the industrial school. Bernstein launches an investigation.
January–February 1952	The Joint Committee to Investigate the Management and Operation of the Arizona Industrial School holds hearings on the Fort Grant scandal. Judge Bernstein and Judge W. E. Patterson file contempt of court charges against Superintendent George Ridgway and members of his staff.
March 10, 1952	*Time* magazine publishes its story on the Fort Grant scandal.
June 9, 1952	The Arizona Supreme Court announces its decision in *Ridgway v. Superior Court of Yavapai County* that halts the proceedings in the contempt trial of Superintendent Ridgway and his staff. Later that year, Ridgway resigns.
November 4, 1952	Republican Barry Goldwater defeats Democrat and U.S. Senate Majority Leader Ernest McFarland.
January 1953	Steve J. Vukcevich becomes superintendent of Fort Grant and fires the remaining staff members accused of wrongdoing. Vukcevich runs the school as a military academy until Arizona converts Fort Grant into an adult prison in 1973.

May 5, 1954	Judge Charles Bernstein announces his ruling in *Heard v. Davis*, declaring that the segregation of African American children in Phoenix's Wilson Elementary School District violates the 14th Amendment's equal protection clause.
May 17, 1954	The U.S. Supreme Court announces its unanimous decision in *Brown v. Board of Education*, declaring that "separate but equal is inherently unequal."
January 1955	Senator Estes Kefauver assumes the chairmanship of the Senate Subcommittee to Investigate Juvenile Delinquency. During the next two years, he holds televised hearings that focus on the relationship between mass media and youth violence.
October 15, 1956	William Brennan joins the U.S. Supreme Court.
September 1960	The Gault family (Paul and Margaret and their sons, Louis and Gerald) become residents of Globe, Arizona.
November 8, 1960	The Democratic Senator John F. Kennedy of Massachusetts defeats Vice President Richard M. Nixon for the presidency. Arizonans approve the Modern Court Amendment.
May 11, 1961	President Kennedy issues Executive Order 10940, establishing the President's Committee on Juvenile Delinquency, to be chaired by his brother, Attorney General Robert F. Kennedy.
June 19, 1961	The Warren Court decides *Mapp v. Ohio*, applying the exclusionary rule to state criminal courts.
September 22, 1961	President Kennedy signs the Juvenile Delinquency and Youth Offenses Control Act.
July 2, 1962	Gerald Gault is accused by another boy of stealing a baseball mitt. The Gila County Juvenile Court informally handles his case, and Gerald is not charged.
March 18, 1963	The U.S. Supreme Court announces its decision in *Gideon v. Wainwright*, guaranteeing the right to assistance of counsel in all felony cases. The Court had appointed Abe Fortas to represent Clarence Gideon, who was indigent. Norman Dorsen worked on the ACLU's amicus brief.

{ *Chronology* }

November 22, 1963	President Kennedy is assassinated, and Lyndon B. Johnson becomes the 36th President of the United States.
February 2, 1964	At the Alden Theatre, eleven-year-old Curtis Uptain steals $60 dollars from Mary Hernandez's wallet. Gerald, who was seen with Uptain, is questioned by the police. Both boys are charged with grand theft and have their cases referred to the Gila County Juvenile Court.
February 3, 1964	Judge Robert McGhee sends Curtis Uptain to Fort Grant on an indeterminate sentence.
February 25, 1964	Judge Robert McGhee places Gerald Gault on probation for six months and orders him to stay out of trouble and to obey his mother.
March 16, 1964	In a special message to congress, President Johnson proposes a War on Poverty.
May 22, 1964	President Johnson delivers his "Great Society" speech at the University of Michigan in Ann Arbor.
June 8, 1964	Ronald Lewis visits Gerald Gault. Gault phones Ora Cook. Afterward, Cook calls the police to report an obscene phone call. Gerald and Ronald are both arrested and charged with making "lewd phone calls." Deputy Probation Officer Charles Flagg is assigned to the case, and both boys are placed in detention.
June 9, 1964	Judge Robert McGhee holds an initial hearing.
June 10, 1964	Paul Gault, who is working on a project at the Grand Canyon, learns that his son has been detained.
June 12, 1964	Gerald is released to his mother's custody. Officer Flagg gives her a note stating only "Mrs. Gault: Judge McGhee has set Monday June 15, 1964 at 11:00 A.M. as the date and time for further Hearings on Jerry's delinquency." That evening, Paul Gault arrives home.
June 13, 1964	Paul and Marjorie Gault ask Chief of Police Rob Weinberger whether they need an attorney. He says that they do not need one because Judge McGhee will only place Gerald on probation for a year.
June 15, 1964	Judge McGhee holds the second hearing. He commits Gerald Gault to Fort Grant on an indeterminate sentence. Gerald is immediately taken away.

June 22, 1964	At the Shoreham Hotel in Washington, D.C., Chief Justice Earl Warren delivers his "Equal Justice for Juveniles" address to the Annual Conference of Juvenile Court Judges.
August 1, 1964	Paul and Marjorie Gault meet with Amelia Lewis in her law office near Phoenix. She takes their case.
August 3, 1964	Amelia Lewis visits Justice Lorna Lockwood of the Arizona Supreme Court to discuss filing a habeas corpus petition. Lockwood arranges for the Maricopa County Superior Court to hold a habeas corpus hearing.
August 17, 1964	Maricopa Superior Court Judge Fred Hyder presides over the habeas corpus hearing. He dismisses the petition.
November 3, 1964	In the presidential election, Lyndon Johnson wins a landslide victory over his conservative Republican challenger, Senator Barry Goldwater of Arizona.
November 17, 1964	Amelia Lewis petitions the Arizona Supreme Court to review the *Gault* case.
November 23, 1964	Gerald Gault is allowed to return home but remains under the custody of the Board of Directors of State Institutions for Juveniles for the State of Arizona.
October 3, 1965	Abe Fortas is sworn in as a justice of the U.S. Supreme Court.
November 10, 1965	The Arizona Supreme Court rules against the Gaults, with Justice Charles Bernstein writing the unanimous opinion.
Mid-November 1965	Amelia Lewis receives permission from the Northern Arizona Chapter of the ACLU and the national board to appeal *Gault* to the U.S. Supreme Court.
March 8, 1966	Amelia Lewis mails the *Gault* file to Melvin Wulf, the National Legal Director of the ACLU.
March 16, 1966	Melvin Wulf sends the *Gault* file to Gertrude Mainzer at the Arthur Garfield Hay Civil Liberties Program at New York University Law School.
March 21, 1966	The U.S. Supreme Court announces its decision in *Kent v. United States*, written by Justice Abe Fortas. Fortas declares that children may be receiving the "worst of both worlds" in the juvenile justice system.

May 2, 1966	Melvin Wulf files the jurisdictional statement in *Gault* with the Clerk of the Supreme Court.
June 13, 1966	The U.S. Supreme Court announces its 5–4 decision in *Miranda v. Arizona*, which holds that police officers must advise defendants of their constitutional rights before interrogating them.
June 20, 1966	The Supreme Court announces that it will hear oral arguments in *Gault* during its next term.
July 20, 1966	Norman Dorsen completes his work on *Political and Civil Liberties in the United States*.
July 27, 1966	Norman Dorsen defends his draft of the Anti-Discrimination Act before the National Conference of Commissions on Uniform State Laws.
August 30, 1966	Norman Dorsen receives James Murray's rough draft of the *Gault* brief.
September 23, 1966	The ACLU files the brief for appellants with the Clerk of the Supreme Court.
October 27, 1966	The State of Arizona files the brief for the appellee with the Clerk of the Supreme Court.
November 8, 1966	Republican Ronald Reagan is elected governor of California, and the Democrat Robert F. Kennedy is elected to the U.S. Senate.
December 6, 1966	The Supreme Court hears oral arguments in *Gault*. Norman Dorsen represents Gerald Gault, Frank Parks defends Arizona, and Merritt Green of the Ohio Association of Juvenile Court Judges argues in support of Arizona.
December 9, 1966	The Supreme Court justices meet in conference to discuss *Gault*.
December 1966– May 1967	Abe Fortas drafts *Gault*.
January 26, 1967	Gerald Gault is granted his "absolute release" from Fort Grant and discharged to the custody of his parents.
February 1967	The U.S. Government Printing Office publishes *The Challenge of Crime in a Free Society: A Report by the President's Commission on Law Enforcement and the Administration of Justice*.
March 17, 1967	Chief Justice Earl Warren sends a note to Fortas, congratulating him on his draft of the *Gault* opinion.

	Warren declares, "It will be known as the Magna Carta for juveniles."
April 4, 1967	Martin Luther King, Jr., delivers his "Beyond Vietnam" address at the Riverside Church in New York City.
May 15, 1967	Justice Fortas announces the U.S. Supreme Court's decision in *Gault*. CBS broadcasts an international town meeting of the world, featuring California Governor Ronald Reagan, Senator Robert F. Kennedy, and foreign college students.
May 27, 1967	The Council of Judges of the National Council on Crime and Delinquency unanimously passes a resolution supporting the *Gault* decision.
October 2, 1967	Thurgood Marshall, who had litigated the school desegregation cases, becomes the first African American justice of the U.S. Supreme Court.
January–February 1968	The Institute of Continuing Legal Education presents three programs on the *Gault* decision. The participants include Amelia Lewis, Lorna Lockwood, Norval Morris, and Anthony Platt.
March 31, 1968	In a televised address from the oval office, President Johnson announces that he will not seek reelection.
April 4, 1968	Martin Luther King, Jr., is assassinated.
June 5, 1968	Senator Robert F. Kennedy is assassinated.
June 13, 1968	Earl Warren writes to President Johnson to announce his intention to resign from his position as chief justice.
June 26, 1968	President Johnson nominates Abe Fortas to succeed Earl Warren as chief justice.
October 1, 1968	President Johnson withdraws the nomination of Abe Fortas to become chief justice of the U.S. Supreme Court.
November 5, 1968	Former Vice President Richard M. Nixon defeats Vice President Hubert Humphrey for the presidency.
May 14, 1969	Abe Fortas resigns from the U.S. Supreme Court.
May 21, 1969	President Nixon nominates Warren E. Burger to become chief justice of the Supreme Court.
June 22, 1969	Warren E. Burger becomes the fifteenth chief justice of the U.S. Supreme Court.

January 20, 1970	The U.S. Supreme Court hears oral arguments in *In re Winship*.
June 8, 1970	Harry Blackmun joins the U.S. Supreme Court.
March 31, 1971	The Burger Court announces its decision in *Winship*. Justice William Brennan writes the majority opinion that determines that criminal courts and juveniles courts must use the reasonable-doubt standard.
June 21, 1971	The Burger Court decides *McKeiver v. Pennsylvania*. Writing for a plurality of the court, Justice Harry Blackmun announces that there is no constitutional right to a jury trial in juvenile court. The decision is the symbolic end of the constitutional domestication of the juvenile court.
January 7, 1972	Lewis F. Powell and William Rehnquist become associate justices of the U.S. Supreme Court.
September 7, 1974	President Gerald Ford signs the Juvenile Justice and Delinquency Prevention Act of 1974 into law. The act sets national standards for juvenile justice policy at the state level.
December 18, 1975	John Paul Stevens joins the U.S. Supreme Court.
November 4, 1980	Ronald Reagan is elected the 40th President of the United States.
September 24, 1981	Sandra Day O'Connor becomes the first woman justice of the United States Supreme Court.
June 4, 1984	The Supreme Court decides *Schall v. Martin*, a case that upholds the constitutionality of a New York pretrial juvenile detention law. Justice William Rehnquist writes the majority opinion.
September 25, 1986	William Rehnquist becomes the sixteenth chief justice of the U.S. Supreme Court.
October 8, 1990	David Souter becomes a justice on the U.S. Supreme Court.
October 22, 1991	Clarence Thomas joins the U.S. Supreme Court.
April 1, 1992	Political historian Barry D. Karl announces, "History is just one damn thing after the next."
August 9, 1993	Ruth Bader Ginsburg joins the U.S. Supreme Court.
November 16, 1994	Amelia Lewis dies at the age of 91.
October 8, 2003	In Safford, Arizona, Assistant Principal Kerry

	Wilson orders a strip search of thirteen-year-old Savana Redding, an eighth-grade student.
March 1, 2005	The U.S. Supreme Court decides *Roper v. Simmons.* Writing for the majority, Justice Anthony Kennedy announces that the Eighth and Fourteenth Amendments prohibit states from using the death penalty on offenders who were under the age of eighteen when they committed their crimes.
September 28, 2005	John Roberts becomes the seventeenth chief justice of the U.S. Supreme Court.
January–December 2007	Children's rights associations and law centers sponsor a "Gault at 40" campaign to raise public awareness about juvenile justice.
June 25, 2009	The U.S. Supreme Court decides *Safford Unified School District #1 v. Redding.* Writing for the majority, Justice David Souter holds that school officials had violated Savana Redding's Fourth Amendment rights. Only Justice Clarence Thomas dissents from this holding.

BIBLIOGRAPHICAL ESSAY

In re Gault has generated an outpouring of scholarship since May 15, 1967, when Chief Justice Fortas announced the U.S. Supreme Court's decision, but this is the first book-length study to place the case in its historical context. There is, however, an excellent young adult account of the case by Susan Dudley Gold, *In re Gault: Juvenile Justice* (New York: Twenty-first Century Books, 1995). For this contribution to the Landmark Law Cases and American Society series, I consulted primary and secondary sources about the case itself; the history of juvenile justice, Arizona, and the Southwest; modern American law and politics; and the U.S. Supreme Court.

Like others who have written about *Gault*—for example, Robert C. Cortner and Clifford M. Lytle in *Constitutional Law and Politics: Three Arizona Cases* (Tucson: University of Arizona Press, 1971); and Christopher P. Manfredi in *The Supreme Court and Juvenile Justice* (Lawrence: University Press of Kansas, 1998)—I started with the U.S. Supreme Court case file. It includes the jurisdictional statement, a transcript of the record, the brief for the appellants, the brief for the appellee, and the amicus curiae briefs. I also examined the Arizona Supreme Court case file that contains Amelia Lewis's filings, correspondence with Arizona officials, and assorted materials from Judge Robert McGhee and the Superintendent of the Arizona State Industrial School. In addition, I listened to the oral arguments before the U.S. Supreme Court, which can be found at the Oyez Project (www.oyez.org).

This book attempts to explain how and why these primary sources were created. Instead of compiling after-the-fact remembrances, I decided to follow the path of the extant primary sources to reach my conclusions. To learn more about the creation of these legal texts, I worked extensively with the ACLU Archives, which are housed at Princeton University and are also more widely available on microfilm. I also used the Norman Dorsen Papers at the Tamiment Library and Robert F. Wagner Labor Archives at New York University Law School and the Abe Fortas Papers, Manuscripts and Archives at the Yale University Library. In addition, I found *The Supreme Court in Conference (1945–1985): The Private Discussions behind Nearly 300 Supreme Court Decisions*, ed. Del Dickson (New York: Oxford University Press, 2001), extremely helpful.

I soon realized that this book would be a biography of a legal case, not the telling of Gerald Gault's own story. I did not, in fact, speak with Mr. Gault, who declined my request for an interview. I did interview Norman Dorsen, who sent me his article, "Reflections on *IN RE GAULT, Rutgers Law Review* 60 (Fall 2007): 1–10; corresponded with Charles Ares; and also spoke with retired chief justice of the Arizona Supreme Court, Frank X. Gordon, Jr., about Arizona juvenile justice and Judge Robert E. McGhee (1914–1982). Gordon and McGhee, as it turned out, were the only members of the Arizona bench who were also licensed vintners. They became friends and exchanged recipes. If Judge McGhee were still alive, I would have contacted him.

In addition to being a biography of a Supreme Court decision, this book is a history of juvenile justice. As I worked on this project, Steven Schlossman and I completed "Juvenile Court," published in *The Child: An Encyclopedic Companion,* ed. Richard A. Shweder (Chicago: University of Chicago Press, 2009), 525–527. Our essay provides an overview of the historiography of juvenile justice. I also wrote "The Elusive Juvenile Court: Its Origins, Practices, and Re-Inventions," published in *The Oxford Handbook of Juvenile Crime and Juvenile Justice,* ed. Barry Feld and Donna Bishop (New York: Oxford University Press, forthcoming 2011). My essay discusses the historical literature that serves as the foundation for this book and provides full citations. The *Oxford Handbook* is now the best introduction to the interdisciplinary literature on juvenile crime and the state response to it. For this book, I also consulted *Justice for the Child: The Juvenile Court in Transition,* ed. Margaret K. Rosenheim (Chicago: University of Chicago Press, 1962), *Gault: What Now for the Juvenile Court?* ed. Virginia Davis Nordin (Ann Arbor, Mich.: Institute of Continuing Legal Education, 1968).

I have also written about the early history of juvenile courts in my *Juvenile Justice in the Making* (New York: Oxford University Press, 2004) and *A Century of Juvenile Justice,* ed. Margaret K. Rosenheim, Franklin E. Zimring, David S. Tanenhaus and Bernardine Dohrn (Chicago: University of Chicago Press, 2002). In these books, I cautioned against viewing the Progressive Era administration of juvenile justice through a post-*Gault* lens because doing so obscures the fact that juvenile courts were works in progress. I also paid close attention to their important role in handling dependency cases and administering social welfare programs, such as mothers' pensions.

Although I became a Nevadan in 1997, I needed to learn more about the history of our neighbors to write this book. Walter Nugent's *Into the West: The Story of Its People* (New York: A. A. Knopf, 1999) provides an excellent overview of the Southwestern migration. Edward Abbey's *The Journey Home: Some Words in Defense of the American West* (New York: Dutton, 1977) was entertaining, and Mona Lynch's *Sunbelt Justice: Arizona and the Transformation of American Punishment* (Stanford, Calif.: Stanford University Press, 2009) was absolutely indispensable. It helped me to conceptualize the first part of the book. Equally important, the two-volume transcript "Before the Joint Committee to Investigate the Management and Operation of the Arizona Industrial School," held by Arizona State University Library, introduced me to desert justice and many of its proponents. I learned about Fort Grant and its troubled history from many sources, including Ralph G. Wales, *The Juvenile Delinquent and the Adult Offender in Arizona: Report of a Statewide Study* (New York: National Probation Association, 1944); Mary Jane Belluzzi, "A History of the Arizona Industrial School," M.A. thesis, Arizona State College, 1949; John Schapps and Milton G. Rector, *Fort Grant, Arizona, U.S.A.: Report of a Survey of the Arizona State Industrial School—1950* (New York: National Probation and Parole Association, 1950); *Correctional Services in Arizona, 1958* (New York: National Probation and Parole Association, 1958); the Fort Grant Centennial Committee, "History of Fort Grant, 1872–1972;" James M. Marlar, "Judge Chambers' Memory Corral," *Arizona Attorney* (December 2008): 25–34; and Karl Jacoby, *Shadows at Dawn: A Borderlands Massacre and the Violence of History* (New York: Penguin, 2008).

Studies of the Arizona bar and bench were also invaluable. *The Superior Court in Arizona, 1912–1984: A History of the Court in Each County since Statehood* (The Arizona Supreme Court, 1985) provides biographies of the state's superior court judges. The Women's Legal History Project, located at the Robert Crown Library, Stanford University, includes two excellent essays on Lorna A. Lockwood that are available online: Angele C. Solano's "Lorna Lockwood: Lawyer, Legislator, Leader" (2001) (http://www.law.stanford.edu/library/womenslegalhistory/papers/LockwoodL_Solano01.pdf) and Colleen Echeveste's "Lorna Elizabeth Lockwood: In Pursuit of the 1967 U.S. Supreme Court Nomination" (http://www.law.stanford.edu/library/womenslegalhistory/papers0203/LockwoodL-Echeveste03.pdf). In addition, Wilbur A. Haak and Lynn F. Haak's *Globe* (Charleston, South Carolina: Arcadia Publishing, 2008) and Stan Watts's *A Legal History of Maricopa County* (Charleston, South Carolina: Arcadia Publishing, 2007) were also helpful. The State of Arizona has also digitized many of its historical records and legal sources and provides access to oral histories online via the Arizona Memory Project: (http://azmemory.lib.az.us/cdm4/browse.php?CISOROOT=/ghmoral). Finally, Liva Baker's *Miranda: Crime, Law and Politics* (New York: Atheneum, 1985) connects Arizona history to national developments in law and politics during the 1960s and 1970s.

As an avid reader of Laura Kalman's work on American law, I drew heavily on her scholarship—*Abe Fortas: A Biography* (New Haven: Yale University Press, 1990) and *The Strange Career of Legal Liberalism* (New Haven: Yale

University Press, 1996)—to frame the second part of this book. And, as I learned in Gerald Rosenberg's 1990 seminar, The Courts as Political Institutions, the national judiciary can do only so much to change local practices. Rosenberg introduced me to the literature on court-ordered reform, including Donald L. Horowitz's *Courts and Social Policy* (Washington, D.C.: Brooking Institution, 1977) and his own *The Hollow Hope: Can Courts Bring about Social Change?* (Chicago: University of Chicago Press, 1991). Christopher Manfredi's splendid *The Supreme Court and Juvenile Justice* builds on these important studies to explain why the *Gault* revolution ultimately failed. I also used standard works on civil liberties, such as Samuel Walker's *In Defense of American Liberties: A History of the ACLU* (New York: Oxford University Press, 1990) and Judy Katalus, *The American Civil Liberties Union and the Making of Modern Liberalism* (Chapel Hill: University of North Carolina Press, 2006). Kenneth I. Kersch's *Constructing Civil Liberties: Discontinuities in the Development of American Constitutional Law* (New York: Cambridge University Press, 2004) was essential reading. I also studied *Political and Civil Rights in the United States: A Collection of Legal and Related Materials*, ed. Thomas I. Emerson, David Haber, and Norman Dorsen (Boston: Little, Brown and Company, 1967), and Norman Dorsen, *Frontiers of Civil Liberties* (New York: Pantheon Books, 1968).

My discussion of modern American politics is drawn from a wide range of studies. I found especially helpful Allen J. Matusow's *The Unraveling of America: A History of Liberalism in the 1960s* (New York: Harper Torchbooks, 1984). Also instructive were Arthur M. Schlesinger, Jr., *The Crisis of Confidence: Ideas, Violence, and Power in America* (Boston: Houghton Mifflin, 1969) and Rick Perlstein's *Nixonland: The Rise of a President and the Fracturing of America* (New York: Scribner, 2008) and *Before the Storm: Barry Goldwater and the Unraveling of the American Consensus* (New York: Hill and Wang, 2001). Sam Tanenhaus's *The Death of Conservatism* (New York: Random House, 2009) and David Frum's *How We Got Here: The 1970s: The Decade That Brought You Modern Life—For Better or Worse* (New York: Basic Books, 2000) reminded me of the importance of conservative ideas. Katherine Beckett, *Making Crime Pay: Law and Order in Contemporary American Politics* (New York: Oxford University Press, 1997); Barry Feld, *Bad Kids: Race and the Transformation of the Juvenile Court* (New York: Oxford University Press, 1999); Miroslava Chávez-García, "In Retrospect: Anthony M. Platt's *The Child Savers: The Invention of Delinquency*," *Reviews in American History* 35:3 (2007): 464–481; Jonathan Simon, *Governing Through Crime: How the War on Crime Transformed American Democracy and Created a Culture of Fear* (New York: Oxford University Press, 2007); Michael Perman, *Pursuit of Unity: A Political History of the American South* (Chapel Hill: University of North Carolina

Press, 2009); Robert Perkinson, *Texas Tough: The Rise of America's Prison Empire* (New York: Metropolitan Books, 2010); and William S. Bush, *Who Gets a Childhood? Race and Juvenile Justice in Twentieth-Century Texas* (Athens: University of Georgia Press, 2010) all helped me to consider the role race plays in criminal justice in modern America.

Writing about the U.S. Supreme Court was the most challenging part of this book. Since reading Bob Woodward and Scott Armstrong's *The Brethren: Inside the Supreme Court* (New York: Simon and Schuster, 1979), I have been fascinated by the nation's high court. To reveal *Gault*'s constitutional significance, I relied heavily on Robert G. McCloskey, *The American Supreme Court* (Chicago: University of Chicago Press, 1960); Anthony Lewis, *Gideon's Trumpet* (New York: Random House, 1964); Walter L. Murphy, *The Elements of Judicial Strategy* (Chicago: University of Chicago Press, 1964); Fred Graham, *The Self-Inflicted Wound* (New York: Macmillan, 1970); Philip B. Kurland, *Politics, the Constitution, and the Warren Court* (Chicago: University of Chicago Press, 1970); Bernard Schwartz, *The Ascent of Pragmatism: The Burger Court in Action* (1990); John W. Johnson, *The Struggle for Student Rights: Tinker v. Des Moines and the 1960s* (Lawrence: University of Kansas Press, 1997); Akhil Reed Amar, *The Bill of Rights: Creation and Reconstruction* (Yale University Press, 1998); Morton Horwitz, *The Warren Court and the Pursuit of Justice* (New York: Hill & Wang, 1998); L. A. Scot Powe, *The Warren Court and American Politics* (Cambridge: Belknap Press of Harvard University Press, 2000); Mark Tushnet, *A Court Divided: The Rehnquist Court and the Future of Constitutional Law* (New York: W. W. Norton, 2005); Peter Charles Hoffer, Williamjames Hull Hoffer, and N. E. H. Hull, *The Supreme Court: An Essential History* (Lawrence: University Press of Kansas, 2007); countless entries from the *Encyclopedia of the Supreme Court of the United States*, 5 vols., ed. David S. Tanenhaus (New York: Macmillan Reference USA, 2008); and Barry C. Feld, "*T.L.O.* and *Redding*'s Unanswered (Misanswered) Fourth Amendment Questions: Few Rights and Fewer Remedies" (forthcoming, *University of Alabama Law Review*).

INDEX

New Jersey Supreme Court, 77
New York
    Juvenile Code, 77, 101
    juvenile courts, 54, 110
    stop-and-frisk law, 62
New York City
    juvenile courts, 65, 108, 118
    pretrial detention of juveniles, 117–120
New York Daily News, 93–94
New York Legal Aid Society, 65
New York University Law School
    Arthur Garfield Hays Civil Liberties
        Program, 49–50, 123
    faculty, 51, 52, 123
Niemann, Joe, 20
Nixon, Richard, 71, 105, 107, 111, 116
Nixon administration, 106–107
NLADA. *See* National Legal Aid and
    Defender Association
North Carolina, schools, 112–113

Obama, Barack, 120
O'Connor, Sandra Day, 117
Ohio Association of Juvenile Judges, 66–67,
    78, 80–81, 90
Ohlin, Lloyd, 51

parens patriae concept
    criticism of, 64
    in juvenile justice, 4, 64, 66, 75–76, 84, 104
    McKeiver case and, 113, 116
    misinterpretations, 104
    pretrial detention and, 118–119
Parks, Frank, 65–66, 67, 78–80, 81
Patterson, W. E., 20, 21, 22
Pennsylvania Supreme Court, 40–41
Phelps, Marlin, 22
Pickrell, Robert W., 36
Pierce, Phillip, 6–7, 11, 18–19
Pima County, Ariz., juvenile court judges,
    13–14
Pima County Bar Association, 27

Platt, Anthony, 103–104, 113, 115
Polier, Justine Wise, 81
Polsy, Leon, 60–61
poverty, 51–52, 79
Powell, Lewis, 116
Presidential Commission on Law
    Enforcement and Administration of
    Justice, 71, 86, 101
pretrial detention, 117–120
prisons
    adult, xv–xvi, 17
    incarceration rate, 120
    See also juvenile correctional institutions
Proctor, Haydn, 77, 84, 88
Progressive reforms, 4–5, 57–58, 66, 75–76,
    103–104
Project on Social Welfare Law, 52
Proposition 101 (Modern Courts
    Amendment; Arizona), 26–27, 39
Puritz, Patricia, 122
Pyle, Howard, 23

Quinn, Terence J., 14

Ramirez, Rudolph "Rudy," 18
Rankin, J. Lee, 54
Reagan, Ronald, 97, 116–117
reasonable doubt standard, 101–102, 108,
    109, 110
Rector, Milton, 7, 8–11, 16
Redding, April, 123
Redding, Savana, 123–128
reformatories. *See* juvenile correctional
    institutions
Rehnquist, William, 62–63, 116–119
Rezneck, Daniel, 63, 72–73, 83, 92, 98–102, 110
Ridgway, George, 6–7, 11, 12, 13, 14–15, 18, 23
Ridgway v. Superior Court of Yavapai County,
    20–22
rights
    civil rights movement, 64–65, 107, 112
    parental, 36